Rivers of Living Water

Rivers of Living Water

How Obtained — How Maintained

STUDIES SETTING FORTH THE
BELIEVER'S POSSESSIONS
IN CHRIST

RUTH PAXSON

MOODY PRESS
CHICAGO

ISBN: 0-8024-7367-9

Printed in the United States of America

CONTENTS

PREFACE

HIGH UP in our Hong Kong Post Office is a text from the Scriptures which runs thus: "As cold water to a thirsty soul, so is good news from a far country," and those Christians in the homelands who (like us in far off China) have been fed for years on the husks of Modernism, will appreciate Miss Paxson's winsome presentation of our living, loving Lord.

Many who attended the conference at which these studies were given, came as water-pots, hoping to obtain sufficient spiritual refreshment to last until the next season of refreshing, but soon realized that what they needed was not a water-pot experience, but wells springing up with waters that would not only supply their own need, but also overflow into "Rivers of Living Water" in blessing to all around.

Many of the missionaries attending the conference had a strong desire that these messages should be printed, so that others might share in the rich spiritual treat set before us by the Lord's messenger.

Miss Paxson, on her return to Shanghai, corrected, and in some measure re-wrote, the copious notes which I had taken, and the studies are printed and published as they left her hands.

In placing this booklet before a wider public I am convinced that God will use it to the deepening of the spiritual life of many of God's children, for seldom, if ever, have we heard or read the Divine plan and purpose for the life of the believer presented so tersely, simply, and clearly, and withal so lovingly and compellingly, as by Miss Paxson on the occasion of this conference.

Multitudes of Christians are living in a dry and thirsty land, not realizing that God has wells of living water that may be theirs for the asking. In the hope that the reading of this booklet may lead all such to be "full unto all the fullness of God in Christ," and in view of the gathering darkness of the apostasy of modern Christendom, these studies are sent out on their mission for the Master.

C. R. WILSON

Hong Kong, China
June 1930

1

THE MARKS OF A CARNAL CHRISTIAN

THERE ARE TWO KINDS of Christians clearly named and described in Scripture. It is of the utmost importance that every Christian should know which kind he *is* and then determine which kind he wishes *to be*. Paul, in I Corinthians 3:1-4, speaks of Christians as either carnal or spiritual.

> And I brethren, could not speak unto you as unto *spiritual*, but as unto *carnal*, even as unto babes in Christ.

> I have fed you with milk, and not with meat: for hitherto ye were not able to bear it, neither yet now are ye able.

> For ye are yet *carnal*; for whereas there is among you envying, and strife, and divisions, are ye not *carnal*, and walk as men?

9

> For while one saith, I am of Paul; and another, I am of Apollos; are ye not *carnal?*

Which kind of Christian are you? Have you ever had your picture taken in a group? Were you eager to see it? And you quickly found the picture *of one person.* If the picture of that one person was good, then the whole picture was good, but, if not, then the picture was poor, and you did not care to own one. Well, tonight, we are going to have a photograph taken of the carnal Christian, and I wonder if you will see yourself in it. It will be an absolutely accurate one because it is to be taken by the Divine photographer who knows each of us through and through.

THE MARKS OF THE CARNAL CHRISTIAN

IT IS A LIFE OF UNCEASING CONFLICT

> For I delight in the law of God after the inward man; But I see *another law in my members, warring against the law of my mind,* and bringing me into captivity to the law of sin which is in my members (Rom. 7:22-23).

> For *the flesh lusteth against the Spirit,* and *the Spirit against the flesh:* and these are

contrary the one to the other; so that ye cannot do the things that ye would (Gal. 5:17).

Two diverse laws warring against one another in the same personality; two forces absolutely contrary to each other, contesting for its control—this is indeed the language of conflict. Two natures, the divine and the fleshly, are engaged in deadly warfare within the Christian. Sometimes the spiritual nature is in the ascendancy, and the believer enjoys a momentary joy, peace, and rest. But more often the fleshly nature is in control, and there is little enjoyment of spiritual blessings.

May I illustrate this conflict which is so common? A friend told me this story of her six-year-old nephew James, who had the bad habit of running away from home. One day his mother told him she would have to punish him if he ran away again. The temptation to do so soon came and he yielded to it. Upon his return home his mother said, "James, didn't you remember that I said if you ran away again I would punish you?" "Yes," said James, "I remembered." "Then why did you do it?" asked his mother. James replied, "It was this way, mother. As I stood there in the road thinking about it, Jesus pulled on one

11

leg and the devil pulled on the other, and the devil pulled the harder!" The Lord Jesus pulling on one leg and Satan pulling on the other is the constant experience of the Christian, but habitually yielding to the devil and giving him the control of the life is the wretched condition of the carnal Christian. Is yours a life of such unceasing wearying conflict?

It is a Life of Repeated Defeat

> For that which I do I know not: *for not what I would, that do I practice: but what I hate, that I do* (Rom. 7:15, R.V.).

> For *the good which I would I do not*; but *the evil which I would not, that I practice* (Rom. 7:19, R.V.).

Romans 7 is someone's spiritual biography. It was no doubt Paul's. But could it not have been yours and mine as well? It is the revelation of a true desire and an honest attempt to live a holy life, but it is surcharged with the atmosphere of deadly defeat; a defeat so overpowering as to burst forth in that despairing cry for deliverance.

> *O wretchel man that I am!* who shall deliver me from the body of this death? (Rom. 7:24).

Who of us has not uttered it? We have made countless resolutions at the dawn of a new day or of a New Year regarding the things we would or would not do. But our hearts have been repeatedly heavy with the humiliating sense of failure. The things we steadfastly determined to do were left undone, and those we solemnly resolved not to do were repeatedly done. Sins of both commission and omission, like evil spirits, haunt our bedchamber and rob us even of the balm of sleep. We have lost our temper, we have been as full of pride, selfishness, and worry this year as we were last year. We have neglected to study the Bible and pray, and we have had no more concern for souls today than we had yesterday.

The trouble is not with the will, for it was very sincere in the decisions made and fully purposed to carry them out.

> For I know that in me (that is, in my flesh.) dwelleth no good thing: *for to will is present with me; but how to perform* that which is good I find not (Rom. 7:18).

But there is a divided control over the carnal Christian's life and that always spells defeat. He may have deliverance, if he will, but it must be a deliverance out of Romans 7 into Romans 8. Is such a deliverance yours?

It is a Life of Protracted Infancy

> And I, brethren, could not speak unto you as unto spiritual, *but as unto carnal, even as unto babes in Christ*. I have fed you with milk, and not with meat: for *hitherto ye were not able to bear it, neither yet now are ye able* (I Cor. 3:1-2).

The carnal Christian never grows up. He remains a mere "babe in Christ." The Corinthian Christians should have been fullgrown, strong, meat-eating grown-ups: instead, they were immature, weak, milk-drinking infants. They did not measure up in either stature or strength to what they should have.

Nothing on earth could be more perfect to loving parents than a baby in babyhood, but oh, the indescribable heartache endured by the parents if that precious child remains a baby in body or in mind! Nothing on earth sets the joy bells of heaven ringing as the birth of one into the family of God, but oh, what pain it must cause the heavenly Father to see that spiritual babe remain in a state of protracted infancy!

Which are you, my friend, a spiritual babe or an adult? To answer this question you may have to answer another. What are the marks of a baby? A baby is helplessly dependent upon others. A baby absorbs attention and expects to be the center of his little world. A baby lives in the realm of his feelings. If all goes well, he is pleased and smiling, but he is exceedingly touchy and, if his desire is crossed at any point, he quickly lets it be known in lusty remonstrance. The carnal Christian bears these selfsame marks.

Hebrews 5:12-14 shows us that the carnal Christian is still dependent upon others. He ought to be far enough advanced to be teaching others: instead, he is still having to be taught, and has not even come to the place where he can take meat instead of milk. He is incapacitated to either receive or impart the deep things of God.

Why were the Corinthian Christians such babes? Paul tells us clearly in the first two chapters of I Corinthians. They were following human leaders, esteeming the wisdom of men more highly than the wisdom of God. They were substituting fodder for food and attempting to satisfy hunger on husks.

The average Christian does not go first-hand to the Bible for food, trusting the Holy Spirit to give him the strong meat of the Word. He is looking only to human teachers for his spiritual nourishment and gulps down whatever they give him. He is a spiritual parasite living on predigested food, consequently he is underfed and anemic. In this weakened state he is open to all forms of spiritual disease. He is an easy prey for temper, pride, impurity, selfishness; and because of his close relationship to other members of the body of Christ, the result is often just such an epidemic of sin as existed in the Corinthian church. Which are you, still a helpless babe or a mature Christian able to be used by God to help others?

It Is a Life of Barren Fruitlessness

> *Every branch in me that beareth not fruit he taketh away*, and every branch that beareth fruit, he purgeth it, that it may bring forth more fruit (John 15:2).

The influence of the carnal Christian is always negative. Because of the inconsistency of his life he is unable to win others to Christ or set a true example to other Christians. He is, therefore, a fruitless branch in the Vine.

16

It is a Life of Adulterous Infidelity

> *Ye adulterers and adulteresses*, know ye
> not that *the friendship of the world is en-
> mity with God?* Whosoever therefore will
> be *a friend of the world is the enemy of
> God* (James 4:4).

This language is very drastic. God plainly
states that any Christian who is a friend of
the world is His enemy, nay even an "adul-
terer" or "adulteress." To realize the force of
this statement one must know what is meant
by "the world." What the church is to Christ,
the world is to Satan. It is his eyes, ears,
hands, feet combined to fashion his most
cunning weapon for capturing and holding
the souls of men. It is Satan's lair for the unsaved and his lure to the saved to keep them
from God. "The world" is human life and society with God left out.

What, then, should be the Christian's relationship to the world? The answer is found in
the Christian's relationship to Christ. Christ
and the Christian are one. They are joined
together in such an absolute identification of
life that the Holy Spirit says the love relationship they bear to one another is analo-
gous to that of marriage.

Is it any wonder, then, that Gods says that friendship with the world on the part of a Christian is tantamount to spiritual adultery? Hobnobbing with the world in its pleasures, entering into partnership with it in its pursuits, fashioning one's life by its principles, working to carry out its program, all make one an accomplice of the evil one against one's own Beloved. Such adulterous unfaithfulness in love marks one as a carnal Christian.

But perhaps you ask, "What constitutes worldliness?"

> *Love not the world, neither the things that are in the world.* If any man love the world, the love of the Father is not in him. *For all that is in the world,* the lust of the flesh, and the lust of the eyes, and the pride of life, *is not of the Father, but is of the world* (I John 2:15-16).

The acid test of worldliness is given here. Worldliness is "all that is not of the Father." Whatever would not be as fitting to Christ's life in the heavenlies as to the Christian's life on earth is worldly.

Worldliness is also "the lust of the flesh," "the lust of the eyes" and "the pride of life."

Worldliness may be manifested in one's conversation, in one's style of hairdress, in one's clothes, in one's friendships, in one's pleasures, in one's possessions, in one's reading, in one's appetites and in one's activities. Anything which feeds or pampers the flesh, the animal part of man, is "the lust of the flesh." Anything that caters merely to the fashions of the world, that stimulates desire for possessions, that keeps the eyes fixed on the seen rather than the unseen is "lust of the eyes." Anything that exalts self, that fosters pride and pomp and that clips the wings of the soul so that it grovels in the dust of earth instead of soaring heavenward is "the pride of life."

Do you love the world and the things of the world? Then you are a carnal Christian.

IT IS A LIFE OF DISHONORING HYPOCRISY

> For ye were sometimes darkness, but *now are ye light in the Lord; walk as children of light* (Eph. 5:8).

> Are ye not carnal, and *walk as men?* (I Cor. 3:3).

The carnal Christian says one thing and does another; his walk does not correspond with his witness. He walks as those who make no profession of being Christian, so he has no power to win them to Christ.

Has God shown you your photograph to-night? Are you a carnal Christian? Do you wish to continue to be one? There is abundant hope for the Christian who, wearied with the conflict, humiliated with the defeat, chagrined by the immaturity, distressed by the fruitlessness, convicted of the infidelity, and pained by the hypocrisy, turns to God and cries out for deliverance from the wretched captivity of carnality into the glorious liberty of true spirituality.

2

MARKS OF A SPIRITUAL CHRISTIAN

As you follow me through the message tonight you will see that the life of the spiritual Christian is in strong contrast to that of the carnal Christian.

It is a Life of Abiding Peace

> Peace I leave with you, my peace I give unto you; not as the world giveth, give I unto you. Let not your heart be troubled, neither let it be afraid (John 14:27).

There is still conflict in the life of the spiritual Christian, for growth comes through conquest in conflict. But there is peace through conscious victory in Christ. The spiritual Christian does not continue in the practice of known, wilful sin, so he lives in the unclouded sunshine of Christ's presence. His communion with the Father is unmarred by the gnawing consciousness of soiled hands, by the pricking of a wounded conscience, or by the condemnation of an accusing heart. So he enjoys abiding peace, deepening joy and satisfying rest in the Lord. Do you have it in your life?

It is Life of Habitual Victory

> But thanks be to God, which *giveth us the victory through our Lord Jesus Christ* (I Cor. 15:57).

Note it does not say "victories" but "the victory." The victory of the resurrection is an all-inclusive one. He, who has ever given you a victory over one sin, can give you the victory over all sin. He, who has kept you from sin for a moment, can with equal ease keep you from that same sin for a day or a month. The victory over sin is a gift through Christ which is ours as we claim it.

> Nay, in all these things *we are more than conquerors through him* that loved us (Rom. 8:37).

It would have been very wonderful had He said we were just conquerors. But He declares we are "more than conquerors." This is victory with a plus sign. This means enough and to spare. This verse tells us we do not have to live on the ragged edge of a victory that we have to strain and struggle to keep.

> Now thanks be unto God, *which always causeth us to triumph in Christ*, and maketh manifest the savor of his knowledge by us in every place (II Cor. 2:14).

Note the word "always." This victory is not restricted to certain times, places and circumstances. God says He can cause us *always* to triumph in Christ. I can almost hear some person in this audience say, "It is all right for you to stand there and preach that such victory is possible, but you do not know what a cantankerous person I have in my family with whom I have to live all the time." No, I do not know the circumstances of your life, but God does and He put the word "always" in that verse. Dare you accept it and believe that God can cause you to "always triumph in Christ"?

The words "habitual victory" were carefully chosen. By "habitual" I mean that victory is *the habit* of the Christian's life. This does not mean that the possessor of such victory is *not able to sin* but he is *able not to sin*.

Continuous sinning will not be the practice of his life.

What is the real, inward meaning of "victory"? Well, it does not mean mere outward control over the expression of sin, but a definite dealing with the inner disposition to sin. Real victory makes a change in the innermost recesses of the spirit that transforms the inner disposition and attitude as well as our outward deed and act. "Real victory never obliges you to conceal what is inside." Many of us do not call sin *sin*. Of course, we are obliged to call some glaring offense against God or man, that becomes more or less public, sin. But what about that black, defiling thing hidden away in the innermost spirit. Is that sin? God says it is.

> Behold, thou desirest truth *in the inward parts*; and *in the hidden part* thou shalt make me to know wisdom. Create in me a clean heart, O God; and renew a *right spirit* within me (Ps. 51:6, 10).

> Having therefore these promises, dearly beloved, *let us cleanse ourselves from all filthiness of the* flesh and *spirit,* perfecting holiness in the fear of God (II Cor. 7:1).

Let us face a few simple tests and see if

we have been "cleansed from all filthiness of the spirit." You used to lose your temper and give way to violent outburst; now there is a large measure of outward control, but a great residue of inward irritation and secret resentment. Is that real victory?

Some one says something unkind or unjust to you; you do not answer back and outwardly you appear polite, but inwardly you are angry, and say to yourself, "I'd like to give her a piece of my mind!" It that freedom from sin?

A sixteen-year-old girl came to a meeting once, where we were speaking of complete victory in Christ. She lived with a cantankerous aunt who was quite addicted to scolding. The girl often tried her aunt's patience by being late home from school. When scolded for it, she always answered back. She went from the meeting determined to be victorious, both in returning from school on time and in answering back, and told her aunt so. The skeptical aunt replied that she would believe in the victory when she saw it. A few days later, she was late home again. The aunt tauntingly said, "Ah, this is your victory, is it?" But not a word escaped the girl's lips. You say "What wonderful victory."

But listen! A few days later, I received an exultant letter from the girl saying, "Oh! Miss Paxson, now I know the meaning of real victory, for when my aunt scolded me I not only didn't answer back but *I didn't want to.*" This is victory indeed.

Some one has wronged you; you do not openly retaliate or seek revenge, but in your innermost heart you wish the person misfortune and rejoice when it comes. Is that having a right spirit?

At a summer conference in China a woman came seeking help. She was unhappy and others around her were made unhappy. There was unlove in her heart; in fact, there was someone she hated. She was a Christian worker, and recognizing the havoc this feeling was working in her own life and in that of others, she tried to gain gradual victories over it. She had hated even the sight of the other person, but she acknowledged finally the sinfulness of that. So she invited the person to dinner in her home, *but hoped she wouldn't come!* Was that victory? When she came to me she had reached the point where she was "*ready to forgive*" but "*would never forget!*" Was that victory? Then she compelled herself to say that she "*wouldn't hate*" but she *"couldn't love."* Was that victory? Not until God, who is love, really possessed her heart did she have God's kind of victory.

Perhaps someone here is saying, "I have experienced occasionally this glorious freedom from some besetting sin, but it has been only a transient liberty. Is there really such a thing here on earth as habitual victory over all known sin?" God says there is.

> If the Son therefore shall make you free, ye shall be free indeed (John 8:36).

> For *the law of the Spirit of life in Christ Jesus hath made me free* from the law of sin and death (Rom. 8:2).

On Calvary's cross Christ died to set us free from sin. To make that perfect victory permanent He has sent the Holy Spirit to indwell and control. The carnal man is under the power of the law of sin. It operates in his life, bringing him much of the time under its dominion. But there is another and a higher law at work in the believer, and as he yields himself to its mighty power, the spiritual man is delivered from the law of sin and death. Herein lies his habitual victory over all known sin. Do you experience such victory?

It is a Life of Constant Growth into Christ-likeness

> But we all, with unveiled face reflecting as a mirror the glory of the Lord, *are transformed into the same image from glory to glory*, even as from the Lord the Spirit (II Cor. 3:18, R.V.).

There is nothing static in true spiritual experience. The upward look and the unveiled face must catch and reflect something of the glory of the Lord. With a growing knowledge of Him and a deepening communion with Him there must be a growing likeness to Him.

On one occasion I was travelling upon the Yangtze River in Central China. A heavy rain-storm had just cleared away and the sun had come out brightly from behind the banked-up clouds. I felt an inward impelling to go out upon the deck and the Lord had a precious message awaiting me. The water of the Yangtze River is very muddy. But as I stepped to the railing and looked over, I did not see the dirty, yellow water that day but, instead, the heavenly blue and fleecy white of the heavens above and all so perfectly reflected that I actually could not believe that I was looking down instead of up. Instantly the Holy Spirit flashed II Corinthians 3:18 into my mind and said, "In yourself you are as unattractive as the water of the Yangtze River, but when your whole being is turned Godward and your life lies all open to Him so that His glory shines upon it and into it, then you will be so transformed into His image that others looking at you will see not you but Christ in you." Oh! friends, are you and I "reflecting as in a mirror the glory of the Lord"?

But there is to be a progression in our likeness to Christ—it is to be *from* glory *to* glory. The spiritual nature is ever reaching out after and laying hold of that which is spiritual in order that it may become more spiritual.

> Every branch in me that beareth *not fruit* he taketh away; and every branch that beareth *fruit* he purgeth it, that it may bring forth *more fruit*. I am the vine, ye are the branches; he that abideth in me, and I in him, the same bringeth forth *much fruit:* for without me ye can do nothing (John 15:2, 5).

"*Not* fruit," "*fruit*," "*more* fruit," "*much* fruit." Do these phrases not unveil before us the potentialities for Christ-likeness open to every branch in the Vine? Do they not also show us the positive progression "*from* glory *to* glory" God expects to see in us? These expressions are descriptive. Which one describes you? Only the *much* fruit glorifies the Father.

> *Herein is my Father glorified, that ye bear much fruit;* so shall ye be my disciples (John 15:8).

But what is the fruit God expects to find on the branch? He tells us.

> But the *fruit of the Spirit* is love, joy, peace, longsuffering, kindness, goodness, faithfulness, meekness, self-control: against such there is no law (Gal. 5:22, R.V.).

The "fruit of the Spirit" is the full-orbed symmetrical character of the Lord Jesus Christ in which there is no lack and no excess. Note it is not "fruits" as so often misquoted. It is just one cluster, and all nine graces are essential to reveal the beauty of true Christ-likeness. But how often we see a great heart of love spoiled by quickness of temper—there is "love" but not "self-control." Or we see a person of great long-suffering but he is also very long-faced. There is "long-suffering" but no "joy." Again one sees a

Christian very long on "faith" but very short on "gentleness." He has more of the thunder of Sinai than the love of Calvary in his make-up. He defends the doctrine with better success than he adorns it. Sometimes we see one whose life is the embodiment of goodness but the goodness is overshadowed by worry and fretfulness. There is "goodness" but not "peace." Oh, how the lack of the excess of any one of these graces mars the symmetry of the cluster! In the spiritual Christian all nine graces blend in such winsome attractiveness that the world sees Christ living within.

It is a Life of Supernatural Power

> Verily, verily, I say unto you, He that believeth on me, *the works that I do shall he do also; and greater works than these shall he do;* because I go unto my Father (John 14:12).

These words were spoken by Christ to a group of unlettered men. One of them was a sunburnt, weather-beaten, rough, old fisherman. He would be ill at ease in a modern college crowd and very probably would fail to pass entrance examinations into a present-day theological seminary. But he belonged to the company of believers to whom this promise was given, and one day it was marvelously fulfilled in his life when through one sermon he won six times as many souls to true discipleship as Jesus did in the three years of His public ministry.

In what did Peter's power consist, and does it avail for you and me? Was it the power of personal charm? of gracious manner? of giant intellect? of eloquent speech? of massive scholarship? of dominant will? While there were many lovable qualities in the impulsive, eager, loving old fisherman, yet none of them could begin to account for such an overwhelming fulfillment of our Lord's promise in him. God clearly reveals the secret of Peter's power.

> But *ye shall receive power, after that the Holy Ghost is come upon you;* and ye shall be witnesses unto me both in Jerusalem, and in all Judea, and in Samaria, and unto the uttermost part of the earth (Acts 1:8).

The power to do "the same works and even greater" is not the power which resides in anything human. On the contrary, it is the power of God, the Holy Spirit which is fully at our disposial when we are fully yielded to Him. Is His supernatural power manifested in your life and works today?

> *For this is the will of God, even your sanctification* (I Thess. 4:3).

> For such an High Priest became us, *who is holy, harmless, undefiled, separate from sinners,* and made higher than the heavens (Heb. 7:26).

The spiritual man takes Christ as his Example, and determines to walk as He walked. Christ lived a life of separateness. He was *in* the world but not *of* it. He had the closest contact with the world but without conformity to it or contagion from it. The spiritual man aspires to a similar separateness of walk.

He bears the same relationship to the world as Christ bore to it, and the world will have the same attitude toward him that it had toward Christ. The Christian will regard the pleasures, pursuits, principles and plans of the world exactly as Jesus Christ did. He was not of the world, therefore the world hated and persecuted Him. So will it treat the Christian.

> *They are not of the world,* even as I am not of the world (John 17:16).

> If ye were of the world, the world would
> love his own: but *because ye are not of the
> world, but I have chosen you out of the
> world,* therefore *the world hateth you.* Re-
> member the word that I said unto you, The
> servant is not greater than his lord. If they
> have persecuted me, *they will also perse-
> cute you;* if they have kept my saying, they
> will keep yours also (John 15:19-20).

God calls you to a life of spiritual "isola-
tion" and "insulation" in order that you may
be more fully conformed to the image of His
Son. Have you responded to the call to come
out and be separate?

It is a Life of Winsome Holiness

> But *like as he who called you is holy, be ye
> yourselves also holy in all manner of living;*
> Because it is written, *Ye shall be holy; for
> I am holy* (I Pet. 1:15-16, R.V.).

Every Christian is called to a holy life.
But many Christians do not want to be holy.
They may want to be spiritual but they are
afraid to be holy. This may be due to mis-
understanding of what holiness is through
false teaching on this subject.

What, then, is holiness? Let us first say

34

what it is not. It is not sinless perfection, nor eradication of the sinful nature, nor is it faultlessness. It neither places one beyond the possibility of sinning nor removes the presence of sin.

Scriptural holiness is not "faultlessness" but it is "blamelessness" in the sight of God. We are to be "preserved blameless" unto His coming, and we shall be "presented faultless" at His coming.

> And the very God of peace sanctify you wholly: and I pray God your whole spirit and soul and body be *preserved blameless unto the coming* of our Lord Jesus Christ (I Thess. 5:23).

> Now unto him that is able to keep you from falling, and *to present you faultless before the presence of his glory* with exceeding joy (Jude 24).

This truth was unfolded to me with fresh meaning four years ago, when I was called upon to dispose of the personal belongings of a dearly loved sister whom God had called home. Among the things she especially treasured was found a letter written to her when I was seven years of age. She had gone on a visit; I loved her and missed her, and that letter was the love of my heart expressed in words. The letter was by no means "faultless," for the penmanship was poor, the grammar was incorrect, and the spelling was imperfect; but it was "blameless" in the sight of my sister, for it came out of a heart of love and was the best letter I could write. For me a grown woman, to write the same letter today would not be "blameless," for my experience in penmanship and my knowledge of grammar and of spelling are far greater.

Holiness is, then, a heart of pure love for God. It is Christ, our Sanctification, enthroned as Life of our life. It is Christ, the Holy One, in us, living, speaking, walking.

Such holiness is winsome, for it spells the holy calm of God mirrored in the face, the holy quietness of God manifested in the voice, the holy graciousness of God expressed in the manner, and the holy fragrance of God emanating from the whole life. Is such winsome holiness yours?

May we bow in a few moments of silence? Which is your life—that of a carnal or a spiritual Christian? If you are not living habitually on the highest plane, will you determine now to do so?

3

TWO CONTRASTING SPHERES

THE FIRST STEP from life on the lowest plane to life on the highest plane is the acceptance of Jesus Christ as Saviour. At the Cross the believing sinner makes a clean-cut separation from the old sphere with all that pertains to it and enters into a totally new sphere of life.

TWO CONTRASTING SPHERES

These two spheres are clearly named and defined.

> For as *in Adam* all die, even so *in Christ* shall all be made alive (I Cor. 15:22).

God has dealt with the whole human race through two representative men, Adam and Christ. Adam is the source of all in the old sphere; Christ is the source of all in the new sphere. By Adam sin entered into the world;

by Christ salvation came to all men; the sinner is in Adam; the believer is in Christ.

"In Adam" we are what we are by nature; "in Christ" we are what we are by grace. "In Adam" we have the life received through human generation; "in Christ" we have the life received through divine regeneration. "In Adam" man was ruined through the first man's sin; "in Christ" man is redeemed through the second Man's sacrifice. "In Adam" all is sin, darkness and death; "in Christ" all is righteousness, light and life.

These two spheres are the exact antithesis of each other, so that life in one precludes life in the other. Every human being is one of these two spheres and his relationship to Jesus Christ determines which one it is.

THE CHARACTERISTIC MARK OF EACH SPHERE

These two spheres may be readily distinguished because each has a characteristic mark.

> For they that are *after the flesh* do mind *the things of the flesh;* but they that are *after the Spirit the things of the Spirit* (Rom. 8:5).

> But ye are not *in the flesh*, but *in the Spirit*, if so be that the Spirit of God dwell in you. Now if any man have not the Spirit of Christ, he is none of his (Rom. 8:9).

The mark of the old sphere is the "flesh" and of the new the "Spirit." The sinner "in Adam" is in the flesh; the believer "in Christ" is in the Spirit. The flesh and the Spirit are mutually irreconcilable enemies in totally diverse camps.

> For *the flesh lusteth against the Spirit*, and *the Spirit against the flesh; and these are contrary the one to the other;* so that ye cannot do the things that ye would (Gal. 5:17).

Man became "flesh" through Adam's sin.

> And Jehovah said, My Spirit shall not strive with man for ever, *for in their going astray they are become flesh* (Gen. 6:3, R.V.).

The flesh is the whole natural man, spirit, soul and body, alienated from God. It is the life of nature, whether good or bad, received through human generation. It is *all* that I am as a son of Adam.

> That which is *born of the flesh is flesh* (John 3:6).

39

God sees nothing good in the flesh. Even the very best product which physical generation can produce He rejects.

> For I know that *in me (that is, in my flesh,) dwelleth* NO GOOD THING: for to will is present with me, but how to perform that which is good I find not (Rom. 7:18).

Paul's estimate of the flesh as here given is God-inspired, as anyone must readily admit who knows his former high regard for himself (Phil. 3:4-6). Through human generation Paul was richly endowed. Paul's "flesh" was educated, cultured, moral, even religious flesh, yet it was wholly unacceptable to God. So there is but one attitude which God can possibly have toward the flesh, which is that of condemnation and rejection. God refuses to deal with the flesh on any terms, for it is irretrievably displeasing to Him.

> They that are in the flesh CANNOT *please God* (Rom. 8:8).

Regeneration opens the way for the believer to enter the sphere of the Spirit. At the new birth the Holy Spirit quickens the human spirit and then makes it his home.

That which is *born of the Spirit is spirit*
(John 3:6).

THE REIGN OF THE OLD MAN

In each of these spheres is a sovereign who
purposes to rule with undivided authority.

> That ye put off concerning the former con-
> versation *the old man, which is corrupt* ac-
> cording to the deceitful lusts (Eph. 4:22).

> Lie not one to another, seeing that ye have
> put off *the old man with his deeds* (Col.
> 3:9).

The sovereign in the old sphere is "the old
man." The very core of the flesh is this sinful, corrupt nature, called "the old man,"
which is a deep-dyed traitor that hates everything that God loves and loves everything
that God hates.

The expression "the old man" is used but
three times in the Bible: in Ephesians 4:22,
Colossians 3:9 and Romans 6:6. It has an
equivalent in the "I" of Galatians 2:20, and
in the word "sin" of Romans 6. The term
commonly used is "self." Through the first
Adam's fall "self" usurped the throne of man's
personality and has held it in its possession,

41

control, and use ever since. Every child is born into the world with KING SELF on the throne, a fact often made evident before he can walk or talk.

"The old man" on the throne determines what the whole life from center to circumference shall be. His evil desires become evil deeds; his unholy aspirations are transmitted into unholy acts; his unrighteous character manifests itself in unrighteous conduct; his ungodly will is expressed in ungodly works. The root "sin" bears fruit in "sins."

DETHRONEMENT OF THE OLD MAN—
CO-CRUCIFIXION WITH CHRIST

The vast majority of Christians stop short in their experience of the blessings of salvation with the forgiveness of past sins and with the hope of heaven in the future. But the present is a forty-year wilderness experience full of futile wanderings, never enjoying peace and rest, never arriving in the promised land.

Few people are willing to admit that "the old man" sits upon the throne and rules the whole being with despotic power. Even among Christians there is gross ignorance of and indifference to the subtle, insidious workings of the old "I." If the grosser works of the flesh are absent from the life, the individual rests in a complacent sense of goodness, failing altogether to apprehend how obnoxious to God are the more refined and less openly manifest sins of the spirit. How few are willing to say, "I know that *in me* dwelleth no good thing."

Let us, then, pause for a moment to take a full-length portrait of this hideous self and see if we are not forced to accept God's estimate of him, and to acquiesce in the method of deliverance from his sovereignty. The foundation of life in the natural man is foursquare: self-will, self-love, self-trust, and self-exaltation; and upon this foundation is reared a superstructure that is one huge capital "I." Self-centeredness, self-assertation, self-conceit, self-indulgence, self-pleasing, self-seeking, self-pity, self-sensitiveness, self-defense, self-sufficiency, self-consciousness, self-righteousness, self-glorying—this is the material out of which the building is fashioned.

Is this delineation of self true or untrue? As we look within our own lives is there one of us who would not have to confess to every one of these hateful manifestations of self at some time in a greater or less degree? We each of us know what a hydra-headed monster that old "I" is. Luther knew it and said, "I am more afraid of my own heart than of the Pope and all his cardinals. I have within me that great Pope Self."

What, then, shall be done with this bold usurper of God's place? God has declared very plainly what He has already done with him. He has but one place for "the old man," and that is the Cross, and but one plan for the termination of his despotic rule, and that is by his crucifixion with Christ.

> Knowing this, that *our old man was crucified with him (Christ)*, that the body of sin might be done away, that so we should no longer be in bondage to sin (Rom. 6:6, R.V.).

> *I have been crucified with Christ;* and it is no longer I that live, but Christ liveth in me: and the life which I now live in the flesh I live in faith, the faith which is in the Son of God, who loved me, and gave himself for me (Gal. 2:20, R.V.).

Two facts are clearly stated here; first that the crucifixion of "the old man" is an already accomplished fact, and, second, that it is a

co-crucifixion. Notice the tenses: "was crucified"—past, and "have been crucified"—past
perfect. The judicial crucifixion of "the old
man" took place centuries ago. Whether or
not a single soul ever accepted this glorious
fact that the entire old creation in Adam was
carried to the cross and there crucified with
Christ, it is as gloriously true as the fact that
Christ Himself was crucified.

Whether from sins or from self, the cross
is God's only place of deliverance. As surely
as Christ "bore my sins in His own body on
the tree" just so surely was my "old man
crucified with Christ" there. If I accept and
act upon the one fact by faith, consistently I
must accept and act upon the other fact by
faith.

Deliverance from the old sphere "in Adam"
and entrance into the new sphere "in Christ"
demands the dethronement of self. No house
can entertain two masters. If the Lord Jesus
is to take the throne and rule over the human
personality, then "the old man" must abdi-
cate. That he will never do. So God must
deal drastically with him. He is a usurper
whom God has condemned and sentenced to
death. That sentence was carried out on Cal-

vary's cross. Now God declares to every person who cries out for deliverance from the tyranny of self, "the old man was crucified with Christ." Do you believe it?

The second fact which these verses make clear, is that it is a co-crucifixion. Our "old man" was crucified *with Christ*. This declares both the method and the time of the crucifixion. There is often confusion at this point. Paul says, "I have been crucified *with Christ*." He did not try to crucify himself nor did his crucifixion take place at some special point in his spiritual experience through some act on his part. It did not take place in Damascus, Arabia, or even when he was caught up to the third heaven. But the death of the old "I" took place on the cross when Christ died there.

This truth becomes easy of apprehension if we but remember that God sees every person either "in Adam" or "in Christ." He deals with the human race through these two representative men. When Adam died the human race died in him. You died in Adam. So did I. Through that spiritual death "the old man" found birth and usurped God's place on the throne of man's life. But Christ came as the last Adam to recover for God and for the race all that had been lost to them through the first Adam. Christ died and the race of sinners died in Him. The old "I" in you and in me was judicially crucified with Christ. "Ye died," and your death dates from the death of Christ.

The perfection of God's grace is marvelously manifested in this glorious fact of co-crucifixion—the sinner with the Saviour on the cross. It needs only the perfection of man's faith to make it a glorious reality in his spiritual experience.

4

THE CHRISTIAN'S CHOICE — SELF OR CHRIST

There are two kinds of Christians, easily identified and clearly distinguished from each other. The question may be asked, "How can there be two streams, from one fountain-head, which flow so widely apart?" We must get an answer to this question if we are to choose to be spiritual Christians and live consistently as such.

The Co-Existence of two Natures in every Believer

Every Christian is conscious of a duality within himself. Part of him wants to please Christ, part of him wants to satisfy every demand of self. Part of him longs for the rest of the promised land, another part lusts for the onions, leeks and garlic of Egypt. Part of him grasps Christ, part of him grips the world. There is a law of gravitation which pulls him sinward while at the same time a law of counteraction pulls him Christward.

The Scriptural explanation of this duality is that every believer has within him two natures: the sinful, Adamic nature; and the spiritual, Christ nature. The first epistle of John gives us a clear unfolding of this truth.

> *If we say that we HAVE no sin*, we deceive ourselves, and the truth is not in us (I John 1:8).

If any Christian, however full-grown, says he has no sin and is entirely freed from his old nature, he deceives himself. He does not deceive his family or his friends, least of all does he deceive God. He deceives only himself. In the next verse God makes provision for the sins of Christians.

> If we confess our sins, he is faithful and just to forgive us our sins, and to cleanse us from all unrighteousness (I John 1:9).

The "sins" and "all unrighteousness" mentioned here are those of saints.

If there is "*no sin*," then the believer "*can not sin*." Every stream, however tiny, must have a source. The apostle John knew well that some people longing after holiness would be tempted to go beyond Scripture, so he uses very drastic language by way of warning.

> If we say that we have not sinned, *we make him* (God) *a liar, and his word is not in us* (I John 1:10).

The gross, fleshly sins may have gone from us, but what of the hidden sins of the spirit; the harsh judgment, the secret irritability, the wrong attitude, the unkind thought? Then what of the sins of omission? I am more afraid of James 4:17 than of almost any verse in the Bible. It tells me that sin is not merely an act or an attitude; but it is *an absence*. It is what I do not do that I know I should do. Who then is without sin?

In every believer is that old nature that can do nothing but sin. Inherent within it is a threefold inability: it cannot know, obey or please God. By physical birth we possess this God-ignorant, God-defying, God-displeasing nature which is bent on the gratification and the glorification of self.

In every believer is a new nature which cannot sin. Inherent within it is a threefold capacity: it can and does know, obey and please God. By spiritual birth we possess this God-knowing, God-obeying, God-pleasing nature which is bent on the gratification and glorification of Christ.

THE CONFLICT OF THESE TWO NATURES IN EVERY BELIEVER

These two natures co-inhabit every believer through life. John wrote to believers as though he did not expect them to sin because they had this God-begotten nature.

> My little children, these things write I unto you, *that ye sin not* (I John 2:1).

Yet he made full provision for their sinning because they had this devil-begotten nature.

> And, *if any man sin*, we have an advocate with the Father, Jesus Christ the righteous (I John 2:1).

God makes no attempt to improve this old nature, because it is unimprovable; nor to subject it, for it is irreconcilable; nor yet to eradicate it, because He has a far more wonderful way of conquest over it.

The co-existence of these two diametrically opposed natures in one person inevitably necessitates conflict. It is the age-long conflict between Satan and Christ, with the Christian's life as the battleground. The conflict is personalized in Romans 7. Christ had come into Paul's life to possess and control it. But another contests His right. Romans 7 is the picture of a Christian torn to pieces by this conflict and baffled and discouraged beyond words.

It is this conflict which staggers many a young Christian and often causes a total eclipse of faith or a gradual backsliding into the world. The first step into the Christian life was taken because his conscience was awakened to the evil of his doings. His chief concern was for his *sins*. He sought Christ as his Saviour that he might have forgiveness of sins. In the realization of forgiveness he experienced great joy and began witnessing for Christ. But soon he finds himself doing the same things again; the evil habits persist; worse than all, joy in Christ lessens, the heart grows cold, and he becomes utterly discouraged.

But his love for God is not altogether quenched. Something in him cries out for God, while another something contests every inch of God's claim and control. He strives against sin, prays for release, and makes every effort in his own strength to get victory. He comes to the place where he says, "Is it worthwhile?" One day on the very verge of despair he cries out for deliverance, "Oh! wretched man that I am, who shall deliver me from the body of this death?"

What seems like his utter downfall is really his hour of deliverance. He had to come to the end of Romans 7 before he could enter into Romans 8. Are you living in Romans 7 today? Do you wish to know the way out?

THE CONQUEST OF THE OLD NATURE

God has given us clear and definite instruction regarding our part in the dethronement of self.

We must condemn the flesh. God condemns the flesh as altogether sinful. He sees "no good thing" in it. We must accept God's estimate of the flesh and act accordingly. This seems easy, but it is very difficult. God's standard is very exacting. He says there is "no good thing" from the center to the circumference of the flesh. He condemns its innermost desires (Eph. 2:3) and its outermost deeds (Col. 3:9). The first step that Paul took to life on the highest plane was to condemn the flesh and "to have no confidence" in it (Phil. 3:3-4).

But we do have confidence in the flesh. We divide it into the good and the bad. Certain things in the flesh we condemn as sinful, others we admit to be weaknesses; but there is another good-sized portion of the flesh that we rate very high and trust without reserve. We make a cross-section of the flesh, good and bad together, and think it measures up fairly well.

But let us put the flesh to a test. Take the most God-like thing in human life, which is love, and place the purest specimen of it in your life alongside of I Corinthians 13, which is God's love. Is it always long-suffering with no trace of impatience or irritability? Is it always kind with no rudeness or harshness? Does it never seek its own through selfishness or jealousy? Does it think no evil but is always without uncharitableness and suspicion? Has your flesh never broken down under this divine test? God asks us to condemn even the cross-section as unclean and untrustworthy.

We must consent to the crucifixion of the

old man. God has already crucified the old man, but we must give our hearty consent to the transaction and consider it an accomplished fact. This was the second step Paul took to life on the highest plane. He said, "I have been crucified with Christ" (Gal. 2:20).

Have you consented to your crucifixion with Christ? There can be no reservations, no holding back part of the price. The whole "I" must be reckoned crucified. God asks you to put your signature to this statement, "I have been crucified with Christ." If you have never done so, will you do it now?

We must co-operate with the Holy Spirit in keeping the old man crucified. What Christ has made possible for us the Holy Spirit makes real within us, but only with our intelligent co-operation. God states very clearly what our part is.

(1) Reckon yourself dead unto sin.

> Likewise *reckon ye also yourselves to be dead indeed unto sin*, but alive unto God through Jesus Christ our Lord (Rom. 6:11).

Through the crucifixion of the old man the believer is freed from sin's power and released from sin's dominion. Every claim of sin has been nullified and he has been made dead to sin. Grace has made this an accomplished fact; faith makes it an experimental fact. Through grace the old man was put on the cross and buried in the tomb; through faith he will be kept there. As the Christian reckons himself "dead unto sin" the Holy Spirit makes it real; as he continues to reckon, the Holy spirit continues to make real.

(2) Make no provision for the flesh.

> But put ye on the Lord Jesus Christ, *and make not provision for the flesh, to fulfill the lusts thereof* (Rom. 13:14).

Yet we daily and hourly make provision for the renewal of the life of the flesh by feeding him upon the things that make fat. We provide for the flesh by the books we read, by the pleasures in which we indulge, by the companions we keep, by the pursuits we follow. Do you spend hours in reading novels and then wonder why you have no taste for the Bible? The Holy Spirit lives on spiritual food. Are you starving your spiritual nature by feeding it on husks? Are you trying to feed the Holy Spirit on the theatre, the cinema, dancing, or bridge? Are your nearest friends such as weaken you spiritually? Is it your aim in life to make money and is all your time and strength bent to attain that goal? Then do not wonder that your spirit is lean.

> For *he that soweth to the flesh shall of the flesh reap corruption;* but he that soweth to the Spirit shall of the Spirit reap life everlasting (Gal. 6:8).

God's law of sowing and reaping in the spiritual realm is as inexorable as it is in the material realm. If we sow to the flesh, we shall reap that which is fleshly. To which are you sowing, the flesh or the Spirit?

> For they that are after the flesh *do mind the things of the flesh;* but they that are after the Spirit the things of the Spirit (Rom. 8:5).

"Mind"—it is a strong word. Upon what things is your mind fixedly set and with what things is it habitually occupied? Do you "mind" clothes or a bank account? We are responsible for the direction that our thoughts take. What things do you "mind"?

> That the righteousness of the law might be fulfilled in us, *who walk not after the flesh, but after the Spirit* (Rom. 8:4).

The world judges a Christian very largely by his walk. But what does the world think of the Christian who walks with it six days of the week and separates from it only long enough to go to church on Sunday?

Perhaps you have taken the first step into the Christian life by accepting Christ as your Saviour. You faced the choice of your sin or God's Son, and you chose Christ as your Saviour. But since that time your life has been one long wilderness journey filled with defeat and discouragement. You are tired of it all and your heart cries out for peace, rest and victory. Are you ready then for the second step? God puts before you another choice— self or Christ? Christ is your Saviour. Will you let Him become your Lord?

Oh! the bitter shame and sorrow,
   That a time could ever be,
When I let the Saviour's pity
   Plead in vain, and proudly answered—
   "All of self and none of Thee."

Yet He found me: I beheld Him
   Bleeding on the cursed tree;
Heard Him pray, "Forgive them, Father,"
   And my wistful heart said faintly—
   "Some of self and some of Thee."

Day by day His tender mercy,
  Healing, helping, full and free,
Sweet and strong, and oh! so patient,
  Brought me lower while I whispered—
  "Less of self and more of Thee."

Higher than the highest heavens,
  Deeper than the deepest sea;
Lord, thy love at last has conquered:
  Grant me now my soul's petition—
  "None of self and all of Thee."

5

CHRIST OUR LIFE

CHRIST DESIRES to be not only our Saviour and our Lord, but to be the very Life of our life. God has made ample provision for this through Christ's resurrection and ascension.

CREATION OF THE NEW MAN—
CO-RESURRECTION WITH CHRIST

Death is the gate to life. Co-crucifixion opens the door to co-resurrection. Identification with Christ in His death and burial is but the beginning of the believer's union with Him in an endless life.

> For if we have become *united with him in the likeness of his death*, we shall be *also in the likeness of his resurrection* (Rom. 6:5, R.V.).

> But if *we died with Christ*, we believe that

we shall also live with him (Rom. 6:8, R.V.).

Identification with Christ in His quickening, resurrection and ascension takes the believer into a new sphere and begins the life of the new man.

> But God, who is rich in mercy, for his great love wherewith he loved us, even when we were dead in sins, *hath quickened us together with Christ*, (by grace ye are saved;) and *hath raised us up together*, and *made us sit together in heavenly places in Christ Jesus* (Eph. 2:4-6).

> And that *ye put on the new man*, which after God is created in righteousness and true holiness (Eph. 4:24).

"Together with Christ" on the cross, in the tomb, in the heavenlies! Thus the exalted Lord is able to share with every Christian the victory of His death, the power of His resurrection, and the fullness of His glorified life.

The New Sphere—The Believer in Christ

The moment a penitent sinner puts faith in Christ as Saviour he steps out of life "in Adam" and enters into life "in Christ."

Through the ages upon ages to come he will be "in Christ." We will never understand Paul's epistles if we do not understand the expression "In Christ." It is the key to the whole New Testament. It or its equivalent is used one hundred and thirty times. These two words are the most important ever penned to describe the mutual relationship between the Christian and Christ.

To be "in Christ" determines the Christian's position, privileges and possessions. For to be "in Christ" is to be where He is, to be what He is, and to share what He has.

To be "in Christ" is to be where Christ is. But Christ is in the heavenlies, so that is where the real home of the Christian is. He is a pilgrim on earth, for his real citizenship is in heaven.

> For *our citizenship is in heaven;* whence also we wait for a Saviour, the Lord Jesus Christ (Phil. 3:20, R.V.).
>
> For *here have we no continuing city*, but we seek one to come (Heb. 13:14).

Your present address is just a stopping place on a journey, yet some of you are planning for your earthly home as though you were going to live here forever. Your heart is set on earthly things instead of heavenly.

> If ye then be risen with Christ, *seek those things which are above*, where Christ sitteth on the right hand of God. *Set your affection on things above*, not on things on the earth (Col. 3:1-2).

Do I hear some of you say, "This is too high a standard for me; it is not only impossible but unattractive. I am on this earth and in this world, therefore why should I not live as though I were and enjoy myself and leave the enjoyment of heaven until I get there?" Such is the reasoning of vast numbers of Christians, and their lives are in full harmony with their reasoning.

Is it not necessary for us to become acclimatized to our eternal home in heaven? If the heavenly atmosphere is stifling to me here, what will it be to me there? If the heavenly pleasures and pursuits are unattractive to me now, what will they be to me then? There is music in heaven, but it is not jazz; there are pleasures there, but not those of the ballroom, the card table or the cinema; there are pursuits there, but not those of making money or a name in society. If my heart can-

63

not stand the higher attitude of life in the heavenlies now, how will it stand it then? It is God's intention for you and me to begin to live in heaven now.

To be "in Christ" is to be what Christ is. Christ, the Head of the body, and the Christian who is a member of that body have one life. The blood of the human body is its life. The blood which is now in my head will soon be in my arm. It is the same blood. So the life that is in Christ in the heavenlies is the same life that is in the Christian on earth.

> Herein is our love made perfect, that we may have boldness in the day of judgment: because as he is, so are we in this world (I John 4:17).

We are so enfolded by the Lord Jesus that God cannot see Christ today without seeing us. This moment as God looks at His Son He sees you and me. And what His Son is He sees you and me to be.

To be "in Christ" is to share what Christ has. All that Christ possesses we possess. Every spiritual blessing in Him—joy, peace, victory, power, holiness—is ours *here* and *now*. If we are children of God, then we are His heirs and joint-heirs with Christ, so that

all the Father has given to His Son, the Son
shares with us.

> Blessed be the God and Father of our Lord
> Jesus Christ who hath blessed us *with
> every spiritual blessing* in the heavenly
> places in Christ (Eph. 1:3, R.V.).

> He that spared not his own Son, but deliv-
> ered him up for us all, *how shall he not
> with him also freely give us all things?*
> (Rom. 8:32).

Do you believe that you are a spiritual
multi-millionaire? Are you living like one?
Perhaps you know some Hong Kong million-
aires. Everything about them reveals the fact
that they are rich. Do you live like a spiritual
millionaire, so that others covet your spiritual
wealth? Most of us live like spiritual paupers.

THE NEW CREATION—CHRIST IN THE BELIEVER

When the Holy Spirit begat in the believer
a new nature, He opened the door to a living,
organic union between the Christian and
Christ. Christ and the Christian are then eter-
nally one. So what is it to be a Christian? It
is to have the glorified Christ in us in actual
presence and power.

I have been crucified with Christ; and *it is no longer I that live, but Christ liveth in me;* and that life which I now live in the flesh I live in faith, the faith which is in the Son of God, who loved me, and gave himself for me (Gal. 2:20, R.V.).

Christ Liveth in Me

Can you say it? Paul could. But note the order of his words. First, "I have been crucified with Christ," then "Christ liveth in me." The dethronement of self precedes and makes way for the enthronement of Christ.

To be a Christian is to have Christ the Life of our life in such a way and to such a degree that we can say with Paul, "To me to live is Christ." This means that Christ lives now in you in Hong Kong as truly as He ever lived in Capernaum or Cana. Does He do it?

To be a Christian means to have the divine seed which was planted in our innermost spirit at the new birth blossom out into growing conformity to His perfect life. It is to be daily "transformed into his image from glory to glory." Are you being so transformed?

To be a Christian is to have Christ the Life of our minds, hearts and wills so that it is He who thinks through our minds, loves through our hearts and wills through our wills. It is to have Christ filling our life in ever-increasing measure until we have no life apart from Him. Does He so fill you?

But I can hear some modern Nicodemus say, "How can these things be? How can I live such a life in my home where I receive no help or sympathy but rather ridicule, and where I have so long lived a defeated life? How can I live a consistent life in my social circle which is pervaded with worldliness and wickedness and where Christ is never mentioned or even thought of? How can I live a spiritual life in a place of business where all around me are living wholly in the flesh? How can I even live on the highest plane in my church when it is worldly and modernistic, and I am unfed and untaught?"

Well, you cannot live this life, but Christ can. CHRIST IN US can live this life anywhere and everywhere. He did live it on earth in a home where He was misunderstood and maligned; among people who ridiculed, scoffed, opposed and finally crucified Him. The whole point of this message tonight is to show that we do not have to live this life, but that Christ is willing and able to live it in us.

This is the truth that Christ taught in germ in His last conversation with His disciples. He had told them that He was going away from them and they were wondering how they would ever live without Him. But He assured them that He would be with them in a spiritual presence far more vital and real than the relationship they had formerly had with Him. The life of the Vine was to become the life of the branches.

> I am the vine, ye are the branches; He that abideth in me, and *I in him*, the same bringeth forth much fruit; for without me ye can do nothing (John 15:5).

After He taught this to them He prayed it in. It was the burden of His High Priestly prayer.

> I have declared unto them thy name, and will declare it; that the love wherewith thou hast loved me may be in them, and *I in them* (John 17:26).

Have you ever pondered the last three words of this prayer? *"I in them."* These simple but significant words breathe forth the deepest desire of Christ's heart in relationship to His own. It is His consuming desire to re-incarnate Himself in the Christian.

Paul laid hold upon this glorious truth and it laid hold upon him. It is woven into the warp and woof of his experience, preaching, and missionary service.

"Christ liveth in me" and "to me to live is Christ" was the acme of his personal experience. There was nothing beyond this for Paul. To him this was life on the highest plane.

"Christ in you" was the heart of his message to the churches. It rang out with clarion clearness in all Paul's preaching and teaching.

> To whom God would make known what is the riches of the glory of this mystery among the Gentiles; *which is Christ in you,* the hope of glory (Col. 1:27).

"Christ in you" was the passion of all Paul's missionary service. Paul had but one aim and goal in every form of work done—that Christ might be formed in every convert.

> My little children, of whom I travail in birth again *until Christ be formed in you* (Gal. 4:19).

Christ is the Christian's center; Christ is

the Christian's circumference; Christ is all in between. As Paul put it, "Christ is all and IN all." Christ is the Life of our life.

> When Christ, *who is our life*, shall appear, then shall ye also appear with him in glory (Col. 3:4).

Is He this to *you?*

A PERFECT ONENESS

The spiritual history of every Christian could be written in two phrases, "Ye in me" and "I in you." In God's reckoning Christ and the Christian become one in such a way that Christ is both in the heavenlies and upon earth and the Christian is both on earth and in the heavenlies. Christ in the heavenlies is the invisible part of the Christian. The Christian on earth is the visible part of Christ. This is a staggering thought. Its plain import is that you and I are to bring Christ down from heaven to earth that men may see who He is and what He can do in a human life. It is to have Christ's life lived out in us in such fullness that seeing Him in us men are drawn to Him in faith and love.

But I can hear a doubting Thomas say, "Except I see someone living this Christ life

I will not believe." Well, I believe because I have seen.

For several weeks I lived in a boarding house kept by a little woman who weighed only eighty-five pounds. She was kept from falling into a heap by a brace worn at her back. She had lived on the third floor for two years with no outlook but the blue sky above and a patch of green grass a few feet square below. But her eyes shone like stars, upon her face was a smile that the affliction and adversity she suffered could not remove, and mirrored in her countenance was a radiance that one never sees on land or sea except where the Light of the world dwells in undimmed brightness. Christ was the Life of her life.

A Christian businessman lay dying of cancer. Friends called to comfort him and they left feeling that they had been taken to the very door of heaven and had seen the King in His beauty. Christ was the Life of his life in sickness as He had been in health.

A young Chinese man who had been converted from a very godless, wicked life, and had been a Christian less than two years, came to call on me one day. After he left a gentleman who saw him for only a brief moment said, "Who was that young man? I never met any one who so instantly compelled me to think of Christ as did he." Christ had become the Life of his life.

Is He the Life of your life? Can you truly say, "Christ liveth in me"; "to me to live is Christ"?

There's a Man in the Glory
　　Whose Life is for me,
He's pure and He's holy,
　　Triumphant and free.
He's wise and He's loving,
　　Tender is He;
And His Life in the Glory
　　My life must be.

There's a Man in the Glory
　　Whose Life is for me,
He overcame Satan;
　　From bondage He's free.
In life He is reigning,
　　Kingly is He;
And His Life in the Glory
　　My life must be.

There's a Man in the Glory
　　Whose Life is for me,

In Him is no sickness:
   No weakness has He
He's strong and in vigor,
   Buoyant is He;
And His Life in the Glory
   My life may be.

There's a Man in the Glory
   Whose Life is for me.
His peace is abiding;
   Patient is He.
He's joyful and radiant,
   Expecting to see
His Life in the Glory
   Lived out in me.

6

THE SPIRIT-FILLED LIFE

WE HAVE SEEN that God's wonderful plan of salvation is absolutely perfect. But we must admit that the vast majority of Christians are living on the carnal plane. So the question arises, "Is God's plan practical?" Is it possible for the average Christian to live his life on the highest plane? Perhaps some of you are saying, "The truth regarding life on the highest plane is Biblical and logical, but it does not match my experience nor that of many Christians of my acquaintance. Is not God's plan of salvation too perfect to be practical in a world like this? Is such fullness of Christ's life possible for each of us?"

Everything in God's Word proves its practicability and possibility for every Christian. Whoever has Christ's life in any measure may have it in its fullness.

> I am come that they might have life, and
> that they might have it *more abundantly*
> (John 10:10).

> For in him dwelleth all the fullness of the
> Godhead bodily and *in him ye are made
> full,* who is the head of all principality
> and power (Col. 2:9-10, R.V.).

John the Baptist, in two wonderful procla-
mations, declared the entire scope of Christ's
work when he said, "Behold the Lamb of
God, which taketh away the sin of the
world," and "He that sent me to baptize in
water, the same is he that baptizeth in the
Holy Ghost." Christ's twofold work was to
take away sin and to baptize in the Spirit.
Part of Christ's work was to bring every
Christian into as definite a relationship to the
Holy Spirit as he has to Himself, although it
was to be a different one.

Christ corroborated John's statement in
two invitations which He gave to sinners to
come unto Him and drink of the Water of
life.

> But whosoever drinketh of the water that
> I shall give him shall never thirst: *but the
> water that I shall give him shall BECOME*

IN HIM a well of water springing up unto eternal life (John 4:14, R.V.).

Now on the last day, the great day of the feast, Jesus stood and cried, saying, If any man thirst, let him come unto me and drink. *He that believeth on me,* as the scripture hath said, *FROM WITHIN HIM shall flow rivers of living water* (John 7: 37-38, R.V.).

Christ promised to bestow a gift upon the one who received Him as Saviour, which would bring perfect satisfaction and sufficiency to him and then through him overflow in rich blessing into other lives. Christ's offer to the Samaritan woman was a gift which would change her source of supplies from a water-pot to a well, and then convert her life into a channel through which rivers of Living Water should flow.

THE HOLY SPIRIT—CHRIST'S GIFT TO THE BELIEVER

What the gift was we are told explicitly.

But this spake he of the Spirit, which they that believed on him were to receive: for the Spirit was not yet given; because

Jesus was not yet glorified (John 7:39, R.V.).

Please note that in this verse Jesus tells us three things:
(1) What the gift was—"The Spirit."
(2) To whom given—"They that believed on him."
(3) When bestowed—"When Jesus was glorified."

His work as Sin-bearer must be accomplished first: then as the glorified Lord He would bestow this wondrous gift.

Further light was thrown upon the nature of the gift in Christ's last conversation with the disciples before His exodus. He told them that He was to live in them as an abiding spiritual Presence; that there would be a divine inflow of Life supernatural in quality and a divine outflow of Life supernatural in power. They were to live as He lived and to work as He worked. To provide power for such a life He promised that "another Comforter" would come to take up His permanent abode in them.

When Christ returned to glory, then He fulfilled His promise and sent back the Spirit. On the day of Pentecost the disciples in the upper room were baptized in the Spirit. From that day every one who has been organically and vitally united by faith with the living Lord has received the gift of the Holy Spirit.

> And as I began to speak, the Holy Ghost fell on them, as on us at the beginning. Forasmuch then as God *gave them the like gift as he did unto us, who believed on the Lord Jesus Christ;* what was I, that I could withstand God? (Acts 11:15, 17).

The moment one receives the Sin-bearer as his Saviour he is in the Spirit and the Spirit is in him. It is impossible to accept the Son and to refuse the Spirit.

> But ye are not in the flesh, but *in the Spirit,* if so be that the Spirit of God dwell in you. *Now if any man have not the Spirit of Christ, he is none of his* (Rom. 8:9).

The Spirit-filled Life

In the divine plan there is as definite a purpose in the gift of the Spirit as in the gift of the Son. Through the Son the sinner has life; through the Spirit the believer has life more abundant. Through the Son the sinner leaves the sphere of the natural and enters the sphere of the spiritual; through the Spirit the believer is lifted to the highest heights of life on the spiritual plane. It is God's purpose that every Christian should live a life of deep, growing spirituality. The Holy Spirit lives within us to accomplish this in three ways. He reveals through the Word the fullness to be had in the glorified Christ; He creates in our hearts a desire for this fullness; then He acts as the channel for its transmission from Him to us.

Romans 7 is the picture of the carnal Christian; Romans 8 of the spiritual. In ten verses in Romans 7 "I" is used twenty-five times and the Holy Spirit is not mentioned once. In Romans 8 "I" is used only twice, where it is needed, and the Holy Spirit is mentioned sixteen times; thus we are compelled to believe that fullness of life in Christ means some advance in our relationship to the Holy Spirit and we are constrained to ask God what it is.

In one terse command God shows us the highest point the believer can reach in relationship to the Holy Spirit.

> And be not drunk with wine, wherein is excess, *but be filled with the Spirit* (Eph. 5:18).

"Be filled with the Spirit." You have Him dwelling in you. But that is not enough. Give the Spirit full right of way, let Him fill you from center to circumference. Permit Him to energize you with His mighty power through filling you with Himself.

"Be filled with the Spirit." This is every Christian's *birthright*. By virtue of the new birth he has the right to such fullness. It is not the privilege of a few but the prerogative of all. Are you despising your birthright, as Esau did his, and selling it for a mess of pottage? Do you care more for pleasure or money or position than you do for the fullness of the Holy Spirit?

"Be filled with the Spirit." This is every Christian's *need*. No one can live a truly spiritual life without the Spirit's fullness. One hundred and twenty were filled at Pentecost, only eleven of them were apostles. Some were women who went back home to cook, to sew, to care for a family; others were men who returned to the field and the shop. The names of only a very few are recorded in the Bible, but I have no doubt that the rivers of living water flowed from their lives into other lives. Do not think you are too young to be filled with the Spirit. It will save you from the years of wilderness wandering of many older Christians. Do not say that you are too old, that the hold of sinful habits is too strong upon you. Give the Spirit a chance. Only admit that to be filled with Him is your greatest need and submit your life to Him and He will do the rest.

"Be filled with the Spirit." This is every Christian's *responsibility*. "Be not drunk with wine." Do you obey this command? Surely you do. "Be ye filled with the Spirit." Do you obey this command? Why not, is it not equally binding upon you? Suppose your pastor were habitually dead drunk. Would your church take any action regarding such conduct? Well, suppose he is not filled with the Holy Spirit and never has experienced such fullness. What is done about it? Is not one command just as binding as the other? And is not God dishonored through disobedience to one just as much as to the other? As no Christian is refused the blessing of such an experience, so none will be exempt from its responsibility. As refusal of life in Christ is the greatest sin of the unbeliever, so refusal of the abundant life through the Spirit is the greatest sin of the believer. The fullness of the Holy Spirit is not optional but obligatory. "They were ALL filled with the Holy Ghost."

"Filled"—"Full"—"Fullness."

"Be filled with the Spirit"—A Crisis.

"Full of the Holy Ghost"—A State.

"Filled unto all fullness"—A Process.

The apostles were with Christ for three years, but they were not filled with the Holy Spirit until the day of Pentecost. This was *a crisis*. But they were filled more than once, until we read of Stephen and of Paul that they were "full of the Holy Ghost." This was *a state*. But there was an inexhaustible, infinite fullness from which they might draw according to their receptive capacity, so there was a continuous infilling. This was *a process*. There should be a definite time when we are "filled" for the first time. But there should be repeated infillings that we may be habitually full and yet ever taking in more and more of the fullness of God. To be spiritual one must be filled and kept filled.

The Threefold Manifestation of the Holy Spirit's Fullness

Sometimes there is great confusion here because one expects a spectacular manifestation of so wonderful an experience. There is also much unscriptural teaching on this subject which is leading many astray. Scripture clearly teaches a threefold manifestation.

The Realization of Christ's Abiding Presence

> That he would grant you, according to the riches of his glory, that ye may be *strengthened with power through his Spirit in the inward man; That Christ may dwell in your hearts through faith* (Eph. 3:16-17, R.V.).

The lives of the early Christians seemed fairly surcharged with a vivid, joyous consciousness of the presence of their glorified Lord. He was very real to them. Is the spiritual presence of the living Lord such an intense reality to you? This is one of the rich rewards of a Spirit-filled life.

The Reproduction of Christ's Holy Life

> But *the fruit of the Spirit* is love, joy, peace, longsuffering, kindness, goodness, faithfulness, meekness, self-control: against such there is no law (Gal. 5:22-23, R.V.).

Compressed into these nine exquisite graces is a marvellous word-picture of the character of Jesus Christ in its essential beauty, symmetry and perfection. Such character is not the product of human nature but the fruit of the divine nature. When the Holy Spirit fills us, He reproduces Christ's life within us.

The Re-Enactment of Christ's Supernatural Power

> But *ye shall receive power, after that the Holy Ghost is come upon you:* and ye shall be witnesses unto me both in Jerusalem, and in all Judea, and in Samaria, and unto the uttermost part of the earth (Acts 1:8).

As He sent His disciples forth to do a supernatural task, He promised to endue them with a supernatural power. All power belongs unto Christ, but He delegates His power to us through the Holy Spirit. Have you this power? Wherever He is in fullness He manifests Himself in power.

The fullness of the Holy Spirit is the only thing that will change a carnal Christian into a spiritual one. On the day of Pentecost the apostles were filled with the Holy Spirit, and a casual comparison of their lives before and after Pentecost reveals a marvellous change. They had had daily companionship with

Christ; He had taught them deep truths and shared His prayer life with them; they had lived for three years under the spell of His matchless personality. Yet witness the failure, defeat and sin, jealousy, ambition, selfishness, pride, cowardice, self-will, self-love, self-seeking—all were there largely as before. But at Pentecost self was dethroned and Christ was enthroned and became the Life of their life.

The result was sevenfold. They became men of perception, purity, passion, prayer, power, persecution and praise. They knew their Lord and apprehended the deep truths of salvation. They became men of pure heart. Pride was displaced by humility; selfishness by love; cowardice by courage; and worldliness by heavenly-mindedness. Within their renewed, satisfied spirits was kindled a passionate desire to win others to the Lord who had saved and transformed them. This sent them to God in prayer which became their chief delight and constant occupation. Prayer released power and rivers of living water began coursing through these purified channels into Jerusalem, Samaria and the uttermost parts of the earth. Such manifest power drew down upon them fierce persecution, but even prison cells could not restrain their songs of praise. Pentecost had changed them from carnal into spiritual Christians. Has it so changed you?

"In him a well."—The Holy Spirit, a well of Living Water, a continuously upspringing fountain, is in every Christian. There is then no need of dearth. The promise is you *"shall never thirst."* Did you come to this conference with a water-pot, hoping to take home a sufficient supply for the coming year but expecting that to grow less and less until driven by excessive thirst you would come next year to be revived again? Why not leave the water-pot here and carry away the well? The Spirit-filled life is one of satisfaction and sufficiency.

"Out of him rivers." Satisfaction in Christ means the overflow of Christ. If there is a divine inflow, there is always a divine outflow.

Is such a life yours? If not, do you desire it? It is for you if you truly thirst. *"If any man thirst"*—this is the simple condition. "If any man thirst, let him come unto me and *drink.*" Drink until you are satisfied, until you are full, yea, until you overflow. The fullness of the Holy Spirit is for every one who thirsts and who drinks of the Water of Life.

7

THE PREREQUISITE TO FULLNESS: *CLEANSING*

INFILLING DEMANDS CLEANSING. The infilling of the Holy Spirit demands cleansing. Two commands given to Christians reveal this fact very clearly.

> And *grieve not the holy Spirit of God,* whereby ye are sealed unto the day of redemption (Eph. 4:30).

Grieve is a love word. You cannot grieve one who does not love you. You can hurt him or anger him but you cannot grieve him. The Holy Spirit is a loving, tender, sensitive Personality. To grieve Him means that we are causing pain to Someone who loves us. How can we know what grieves Him? By His names which indicate His nature.

He is the Spirit of *truth* (John 14:17), so

anything false, deceitful, hypocritical, grieves Him. In a meeting I gave the opportunity for testimony. A woman confessed a lie that had been in her life for twelve years. She had coveted the skirt of a friend. Her mother was unwilling to give her the money to buy one like it. So she stole a piece of her mother's jewelry, sold it, bought a skirt and then lied to her mother. Is there a lie in your life? Then do not expect to be filled with the Spirit of truth until your heart is cleansed.

He is the Spirit of *faith* (II Cor. 4:13), so doubt, unbelief, distrust, worry, anxiety, grieve Him. Do you doubt His Word? Is there unbelief regarding the fundamental truths of salvation? Do you worry over your business, your children, your health? If so, you are grieving the Spirit of faith and He cannot fill you.

He is the Spirit of *grace* (Heb. 10:29), so that which is hard, bitter, ungracious, unthankful, malicious, unforgiving, grieves Him. Is there anybody whom you will not forgive or to whom you will not speak? Is there someone with whom you have quarrelled? Is there bitterness in your heart toward God? Do you spend your days in murmuring against your circumstances? Then do not pray to be filled with the Spirit unless you are willing to be cleansed.

He is the Spirit of *holiness* (Rom. 1:4), so anything unclean, defiling, or degrading grieves Him. Do you harbor unclean thoughts? Do you read unclean books? Do you have degrading pictures hung in your home? Do you listen to unclean stories? If so, you are grieving the Holy Spirit.

He is the Spirit of *wisdom* (Eph. 1:17), so ignorance, conceit, arrogance, and folly grieve Him. The Holy Spirit stands ready to teach us and to reveal the deep things of the Word to us. Our ignorance of the Bible, our pride in our own knowledge and ability and our foolish ways, grieve Him.

He is the Spirit of *power, love* and *discipline* (II Tim. 1:7), so our weakness, fruitlessness, disorderliness, and lack of control grieve Him. There are thousands of people all around you who are still unsaved and who do not know the gospel. Perhaps some of these are in your family. Why cannot Christ win them? Because the channels through which His power should flow are choked with sin. Are you embittered because you have been wronged and is your life poisoned by hatred? Do you give way constantly to your bodily appetites, your fleshly desires and temperamental weaknesses? All this grieves the Holy Spirit.

He is the Spirit of *life* (Rom. 8:2), so anything that savors of indifference, lukewarmness, dullness or deadness grieves Him. Do you go for days without opening your Bible? Do you prefer the haunts of pleasure to the house of prayer? This grieves this wonderful Spirit of life.

He is the Spirit of *glory* (I Pet. 4:14), so that which is worldly, earthly, or fleshly grieves Him. Are you carnally minded? Do you love the world? Is your heart set upon the things of earth? This grieves the Holy Spirit.

He dwells within to enable us "to grow up into Christ in all things"; and to bring us daily "into conformity to His image." So anything in us which hinders Him from carrying out this purpose grieves Him. Knowingly to permit anything which is contrary to what the Holy Spirit Himself is, to remain in your life must mean that you love sin more than you love Him. Such unfaithfulness grieves Him.

Spirituality depends upon an harmonious relationship with the Holy Spirit. To indulge known sin means that we are living with a grieved Spirit. To be filled one must be cleansed. "God does not require golden vessels, neither does He seek for silver ones, but He must have clean ones."

Quench not the Spirit (I Thess. 5:19).

We "grieve" the Spirit when we say "Yes" to Satan when he lures us into sin. We "quench" the Spirit when we say "No" to God when He woos us into sanctification and service. To bring the believer wholly into the will of God is, perhaps, the Holy Spirit's hardest task. Self-will is latent in every one of us and is always bursting out into rebellion. The only cure for it is a deliberate choice to do God's will in all things, at all times, and at all costs. It is to have one's heart firmly fixed upon the doing of God's will as the rule for daily life and to permit no exception to the rule.

To grieve or to quench the Spirit is sin. He dwells within us to purify and cleanse us. In a darkened room there would be much of dirt which would pass unnoticed, but when the doors and windows are opened and the sun shines in, even the dust is revealed. The Holy Spirit brings out into the light the sin in our lives, and the more completely He fills us the more perfect will be the revelation and recognition of sin. The nearer God comes to us the more sensitive to sin are we made. Some things which a year ago or even a month ago you would not have called sin you now acknowledge to be sin.

THE MEANS OF CLEANSING

For sinner and saint alike nothing but the blood of Jesus suffices to cleanse from sin.

> *The blood of* Jesus Christ his Son *cleanseth us* from all sin (I John 1:7).

The Christian is in constant contact with sin and the very tense of the verb shows that he never gets beyond the need of the cleansing blood of Christ.

THE METHOD OF CLEANSING

The grieved Holy Spirit will tell us what grieves Him, will point us to I John 1:9, and then our responsibility begins. God requires but one thing of us—a frank, full confession prompted by a true heart repentance.

> *If we confess our sins,* he is faithful and
> just to forgive us our sins, and *to cleanse
> us from all unrighteousness* (I John 1:9).

God will accept no substitute for confession and He instantly detects a counterfeit. Have you ever thought that God would accept from you a larger gift of money, greater activity in service, or a longer prayer in lieu of a confession of sin? Or are you self-deceived in thinking that regret because of suffering for the punishment of sin, or a forced acknowledgment of some offense with no heart sorrow for the sin itself is confession? Sometimes a supposed confession is a confession of the other fellow's sin and a justification of oneself. Oftentimes a confession is but a partial one. Some *top* sin is mentioned while the *root* sin is altogether unconfessed.

In a small meeting of Christian women I once gave the opportunity for confession of sin. A Bible woman quickly spoke, evidently to set a good example to others. She confessed to laziness. I knew that this was not the root sin that needed to be confessed, because she had enjoyed doing it altogether too much. I prayed that night that God would convict her of hypocrisy and lead her to make a true confession. The next day, out of a truly contrite heart, she confessed that she hated the pastor's wife and had not spoken to her for eight years.

Some sins need to be confessed only to God because against Him only have we sinned (Ps. 51:4). Other sins need to be confessed to individuals against whom we have sinned (Jas. 5:16), and again a public confession of sin is sometimes necessary when the whole company of God's people have been wronged (Josh. 7:19-25).

THE MEASURE OF CLEANSING

The cleansing must be from all defilement of both flesh and spirit. Separation from every defiling thing is God's requirement.

> Having therefore these promises, dearly beloved, *let us cleanse ourselves from all filthiness of the flesh and spirit*, perfecting holiness in the fear of God (II Cor. 7:1).

God demands a cleansing that reaches from the innermost desire to the outermost deed; that goes from the core to the circumference of our lives. He asks us to take His conception of sin which regards a lustful look

94

as truly sin as a lustful act; which sees a murderer in the one in whose heart there is hatred as truly as in the one in whose hand there is a bloodstained daggar.

Do you resemble the Pharisees of old who were like whited sepulchres, which appeared beautiful outwardly, but within were full of uncleanness? God commands us to cleanse both the inside and the outside. Is there a root sin in your life that has been there for years? Roots multiply and spread. There is then a trail of sin marking the path of your life since. You must go back over it, claiming cleansing for all sin.

God's withholding of His presence in power from His own children until sin is put away is very strikingly revealed in His dealings with the children of Israel over Achan's sin. God had told them that, when Jericho was taken, no one was to take any of the spoils for himself. But Achan, coveting gold, silver and a Babylonish garment, took them and hid them under his tent. No eye but that of the all-seeing God saw it done. Immediately afterward Israel met with overwhelming defeat at Ai. Joshua, falling upon his face in prayer, charged God with blame for such humiliation before their enemies. But God commanded Joshua to stop praying. He told him that he would not presence Himself with power in their midst so long as the accursed thing was there. The man who had coveted, stolen and lied must be found and confession of sin made.

Is there an Achan in your church who hinders the manifestation of God's power? Are you the man? Have you been praying fervently for the fullness of the Holy Spirit while all the time there has been the continued indulgence of some known sin, the willful disobedience of some known command, or the deliberate resistance to God's clearly revealed will? If so, God is saying to you, "Get thee up, wherefore liest thou upon thy face? Thou hast sinned, neither will I be with you any more except ye destroy the accursed from among you. Up, sanctify yourselves, thou canst not stand before thine enemies until ye take away the accursed thing from among you" (Josh. 7:10-13). So long as you are living with a grieved or a quenched Spirit you cannot be filled. To be filled one must be cleansed.

8

THE BELIEVER'S PART IN BECOMING SPIRITUAL: *YIELDING*

IN THE TWO WONDROUS GIFTS of His Son and His Spirit God has given us all we need to enable us to live on the highest plane. When He gave His Son and His Spirit He gave all that He has to give.

God has made the provision, but you must make the decision whether you will be Spirit-filled or not. There is a boundary line, the right of every man to will, beyond which even God cannot go. God has set a feast before you, but He cannot compel you to eat. He has opened the door into the abundant life, but He cannot compel you to enter. He places in the bank of God a deposit that makes you a spiritual multimillionaire, but

He cannot write your checks. God has done His part, now you must do yours.

The responsibility for fullness or lack of fullness is now in your hands. God is hindered by one thing only—the room that you give Him to fill. You have a clearly defined part in becoming spiritual which we will now consider.

YIELDING—THE BELIEVER'S PART IN BEING SPIRIT-FILLED

The basic principle in a spiritual life lies in its control. The Holy Spirit works to bring the Christian to refuse the further reign of self and to choose the sovereignty of Christ over his life by yielding to Him as Lord.

> Know ye not, that *to whom ye yield yourselves servants to obey*, his servants ye are to whom ye obey; whether of sin unto death, or of obedience unto righteousness? (Rom. 6:16).

To yield the life unconditionally to Christ is the first step in a walk in the Spirit.

THE YIELDED LIFE—WHY?

There is a basic motive in yielding the life

to Christ which when discovered is both convincing and compelling. In the hope that it may help some of you, may I tell you how God led me to this discovery.

I was no older than some of the boys and girls here tonight when I accepted Christ as my Saviour. I experienced deep and real joy in the consciousness of forgiveness of sins and in the fellowship of Christ. This made me desire the salvation of others in my family and for this I prayed, but my prayer was not answered. This troubled me.

Though born again, some of the old sins continued to manifest themselves in the same old way. The outstanding sin in my life was a terrible temper. I would not like to tell you some of the things that I said and did when I lost my temper. Having what often accompanies a quick temper, a sensitive, affectionate heart, I would go apart after an outburst and cry as though my heart would break. Then I would resolve to conquer it by will power, but all to no avail, for my temper was quick and my will was slow. From childhood there is one thing that I have always hated—hypocrisy. I had detected it very easily in other Christians' lives and had criticized them freely for it. But one day God let His own light flood my soul and revealed to me the hypocrisy in myself. Truly loving my Lord, I hated myself for the caricature of Him I was giving to others.

Utterly disheartened I sought the quiet of my own room one day, and determined to stay there until something happened. I told the Lord that either He must show me what a truly Christian life was, and *how* to live it, or I would ask the pastor to take my name from the church roll, that I might tell my family and friends that I no longer made any profession of being a Christian. God knew that I was honest and He always goes nine-tenths of the way to meet an honest soul.

Through two verses from His own Word He answered my questions and liberated my soul. If these two verses could mean as much to even one person here as they meant to me that day, I would praise God throughout all eternity for the privilege of giving them to you tonight.

> What? know ye not that your body is the temple of the Holy Ghost which is in you, which ye have of God, and *ye are not your own? For ye are bought with a price:* therefore glorify God in your body, and in

your spirit, which are God's (I Cor. 6:19-20).

Through three statements in these verses God revealed to me the basic motive in a yielded life.

First, "Know ye not that your body is the temple of the Holy Ghost which is in you?" No, I did not know that my body had any relationship whatever to my conversion nor did I know that the Holy One dwelled within it; that God laid claim to my body, and that the Holy Spirit *had already* made it His home was to me a startling revelation. What kind of dwelling-place was I asking that Holy One to live in?

Suppose you heard today that the greatest ruler on earth was coming to Hong Kong to spend a few days and that the committee on entertainment had chosen your home as the place in which he would stay. What a house-cleaning would take place! What preparation would be made that everything would be fitting and worthy of so honored a guest! But oh! what an unclean, unfit place we ask the King of kings and Lord of lords to live in, not for a day but for a lifetime!

But I said, "Lord, I have given you my

soul, why do I also need to give my body?" I saw faintly that day, but with growing clearness every day since, why God asks for our bodies. He needs a channel for a revelation of Himself to the world. "The Word was made flesh and dwelt among us" and men saw the Father in the Son. Christ is now in heaven. But oh! isn't His presence needed here on earth? Do not those in your city, home, school, office need to see Him? In what way will He reveal Himself to men now? He has two ways.

One is through His Word. But how many millions do not possess a Bible? How many other millions could not read it if they did? The other way is through us Christians who form His body on earth. Oh! the greatest need in Hong Kong today is not merely preaching and teaching the gospel, but it is to see Jesus Christ walking up and down these streets and living in your homes. How will He do it? Through you. The Lord Jesus showed me that day that He needed my body as a medium of revelation of Himself.

There was a marvelously convincing appeal in this to me, yet I refused to yield. Was my life not my own? Was it not asking too much to turn over its absolute sovereignty to another? Was it safe? Was it reasonable? Was it needful? Oh! the plausible arguments Self advanced to retain the kingship over my life!

But my Lord had anticipated this and was prepared to meet it by that second wonderful statement. "What? Know ye that ye are not your own?" If everything else is forgotten this evening, I pray that this question will be embedded deep within your heart. It was like a sharp two-edged sword which penetrated to my innermost being and lodged there. How these words brought to light the hypocrisy of professing that I belonged to Christ while Self still retained the reins of government! How they went straight to the very heart of the issue like an axe laid at the root of the tree—the enthronement of Christ as Lord over my life or the continued reign of Self!

But if I yielded, what might Christ not ask of me or take from me? I would have been glad to turn over to the Lord all the unpleasant, unmanageable parts of my life if He would only leave all the rest to me. To master my will He had to melt my heart.

"What? Know ye that ye are not your own, *for ye are bought with a price?*" Bought! Not my own because—bought! I had thought that by yielding I would be conferring the ownership of my life upon Christ. But that day God revealed to me that *I already belonged to Christ* by the right of purchase and that Christ's claim to the undivided possession and control of my life was an absolutely legitimate one.

This claim I had to admit, but still I would not yield. How patient He was with my incredible stubbornness! Very tenderly He opened my eyes and illuminated them that I might see Christ crucified. "Bought *with a price*"! Oh! THAT PRICE! "Redeemed—with the precious blood of Christ!" This the price paid for me! The life of the spotless, stainless Son of God laid down for my sinful, selfish life! That day I saw a Saviour dying for a sinner! A Life given for a life!

Up to that time I had been saying, "*Must I give myself to Him?*" But that day I cried, "Lord, may I give myself to Thee?" and I yielded all that I was and all that I had to Christ for time and for eternity.

And what was the basic motive in that act of yielding? It was just the joyous response of love to Love following the spiritual apprehension of the reasonableness and rightfulness of Christ's claim upon my life. Then may I define yielding. Yielding is the definite, vol-

untary transference of the undivided possession, control and use of the whole being,
spirit, soul and body, from Self to Christ, to
whom it rightfully belongs by creation and
by purchase.

It is not in order to be His, but because we
are His, that we yield our lives to Him. Purchase gives title to property, but it is only delivery that gives possession. In Peking there
was a girls' school which grew in numbers so
that additional buildings were needed. These
were purchased from a Chinese family whose
property adjoined the school. After much
bargaining a sale was effected. The papers
were drawn up and the purchase price paid.
But in the fall the school was unable to oc-
cupy and use the buildings. Why not? *The
Chinese family had not moved out*. Purchase
gives title, but only delivery gives possession.

On the cross, through His shed blood, Christ
paid the price for the possession of your life.
It is His by right of purchase. But have you
delivered unto Him that which is His? Have
you moved out so that He may move in?

Christ has the right to exempt you from
His property, for He *is* Lord. But His way is
to constrain by love rather than conquer by
force. So He appeals to us thus, "I beseech

you by the mercies of God that ye present your bodies a living sacrifice." What response have you made to this appeal?

THE YIELDED LIFE. WHAT?

Self will relinquish nothing except under compulsion. So it is necessary to understand the full measurement of a yielded life. Many of us think that God wants *things* from us. God is a Person: what He desires most is fellowship with a person, so He wants *us*. He asks first that we yield *ourselves*.

> And this they did, not as we hoped, but *first gave their own selves to the Lord*, and unto us by the will of God (II Cor. 8:5).

But God specifies the measurement a bit more explicitly lest we stop short with merely "giving our heart to the Lord" or "the saving of our soul." It is the easiest thing in the world to use the phraseology of consecration while missing the reality of it. God asks for the body as well as spirit and soul.

> *I beseech you therefore, brethren, by the mercies of God, that ye present your bodies* a living sarcifice, holy, acceptable unto God, *which is your reasonable service* (Rom. 12:1).

But God goes still further, for He leaves no loophole in this matter of yielding. He knows full well how the beauty of a life may be marred and its testimony nullified by the unyieldedness of even one member of the body. What a source of evil is an unyielded tongue! What possibilities for covetousness in an unyielded eye! What paths of wickedness are open before unyielded feet! What a catch-all for gossip is an unyielded ear! God specifies the measurement of surrender, and it reaches out to include every member of your body.

> Neither yield ye your members as instruments of unrighteousness unto sin: *but yield yourselves unto God,* as those that are alive from the dead, and your members as instruments of righteousness unto God (Rom. 6:13).

> "Yourselves,"
> "Your bodies,"
> "Your members."

It is all-inclusive. Nothing is omitted or exempt. God has sanctified our whole personality. Our consecration should be the counterpart of His sanctification.

> And *the very God of peace sanctify you wholly;* and I pray God *your whole spirit soul and body be preserved blameless* unto the coming of our Lord Jesus Christ (I Thess. 5:23).

Our yielding to Christ then includes everything *within*—intellect, heart, will; and everything *without*—home, children, business, possessions, pleasures, friendships, time, money and life plus. It includes everything in our past, present and future. Sometimes it is easy to surrender the past, but distrust His keeping power for the present and we are full of fear for the future. It includes our worst and our best. Perhaps we gladly give over the dregs of our life to Christ but we wish to keep the cream for ourselves.

But in taking the measure of our yielding let it be clearly understood there can be no reservations. We cannot set apart any part of our lives and earmark it "Reserved." The refusal to yield any part is an act of rebellion against God. If Christ is to be Lord, He must be Lord of all.

The Yielded Life. How?

God, in His infinite grace, always takes the

iniative in bringing us into a fuller experience of our inheritance in Christ. So the Lord Jesus stands outside the door of every unyielded room in your life seeking entrance. If He enters, the door must be opened from the inside.

> Behold, I stand at the door, and knock: *If any man hear my voice, and open the door,* I will come in to him, and sup with him, and he with me (Rev. 3:20).

He stands and knocks, "If any man hear my voice." Have you heard it tonight? "And open the door." Oh! here is the "How" of yielding. It is just opening the door. Have you done it? Let us state clearly what this involves.

Yielding to Christ is a *definite* act. It is not an oft-repeated wish that stops in mere desire, but it is a decisive act of the will. Desire becomes decision and decision crystallizes into action. You must say, "I *do* here and now yield myself unreservedly to Christ."

Yielding to Christ is a *voluntary* act. He stands outside the door but He does not force the lock. He waits for you to open the door. It is Love that desires to enter, but unless met by love, the entrance would bring heartache rather than joy. With a smile and a song He wants you to open the door.

Yielding to Christ is a *final* act. If your yielding is such as I have described tonight, then such an act need never be repeated. If done honestly, it is for time and for eternity. Through yielding you have acknowledged that you are not your own, you have transferred the ownership of your life to Christ, you have crowned Him Lord, and you have placed yourself wholly under His sovereign control. To repeat this initial act implies dishonesty and falseness in ever having done it.

Of course, one does not know at the time of yielding all that is involved in that act or all that it will require of him. It is only after you begin to live wholly for God that you will understand the terrible hold of Self upon your life. But the Holy Spirit will faithfully reveal this. What must one do as these revelations come? Does he need to yield his life all over again? No, that was done once and for all. Simply say, "Lord, this thing was *part* of that whole which I yielded to thee. It, too, belongs to that initial surrender. I did not see until now that it is still unyielded. Just now I yield *this particular thing* to thee." Thus *the initial act* of yielding becomes a *continuous attitude.* "Surrender is a crisis that develops into a process."

From the human standpoint, the first condition for a life lived on the highest plane is the yielding of the life to Christ. Have you yielded? Is every door unlocked and open to Christ your Lord? I once visited a college town to lead evangelistic meetings. Upon arriving at the home where I was to be entertained my hostess took me by an outside stairway to the guest-room, which was over the kitchen. She then left home for the day. Soon I heard someone at thhe front door and I thought it was probably the man who was to bring my trunk. As it was raining very hard, I decided to have the trunk put inside downstairs. There were three doors leading into the house from the back porch. I went to the first and tried to open it but could not— it was locked. I tried the second and the third, but each was locked.

Suddenly seized with a strange sense of aloneness I rushed upstairs to the little backroom guest chamber—the only room in the house open to me. To be a bit more conscious of Christ's companionship, I dropped to my knees in prayer. Instantly He spoke to me, saying, "Do you not know that is the way thousands of people treat Me? They invite Me into their lives and then put Me away in a little back guest chamber and there expect Me to stay. But I long to enter into every room of their lives and share all their experiences."

Oh! friends, where have you put Christ in your life? Have *you* any locked doors? Has He put His nail-pierced hand on the pleasure room of your life and longed to enter it but found it locked from the inside? Has He wanted to enter into the room where your business was carried on and share in both its projects and profits? Has He been denied entrance because shady, crooked practices went on there which His all-seeing eye would detect? Has He longed to enter into the room where life plans were being shaped and to help in the fashioning of them? And He tried the door, but entrance was denied— locked from the inside! And has He who longs to fill and to bless you gone back to His little upstairs back room with a grieved and sorrowful heart?

I went from that college town to another. My hostess there was a dear widow. Her home was very humble. We ate in the kitchen, but oh! such hospitality I have seldom enjoyed. Every good thing which her frugal means would permit her to provide she had for me. The first day she said to me, "Miss Paxson, my home is very humble, but while you are here it is all yours. Go where you want to and do just what you want to—just make yourself at home." And I, who traveled constantly, oh! how I spread out over that whole house and made it mine the few days I was there!

Oh! friends, is the Lord Jesus living within you? Have you ever said to Him, "Lord Jesus, I have only a very simple life to offer you as a dwelling-place, but while you are here *it is all yours*. Go where you want to, do what you want to—*just make yourself at home!*" He waits for just such an invitation. How quickly He will accept it when once honestly offered, and how He will spread out over the whole life—truly making Himself at home. If you have not unlocked all the doors from the inside and given Him a gracious and glad invitation to enter, will you do so tonight?

9

THE BELIEVER'S PART IN BECOMING SPIRITUAL: *FAITH*

SOME HERE MAY SAY "As far as I know I have yielded my life wholly to Christ, yet I still seem to be living on the plane of the carnal Christian. Is it possible to be yielded and yet not filled with the Holy Spirit?" Yes, the emptied life waits for faith to claim the fullness.

Surrender says, "Lord, I am not my own. I present my body a living sacrifice." Faith says, "Christ liveth in me." Surrender says, "Lord, what wilt Thou have me to do?" Faith says, "I can do all things through Christ which strengtheneth me." Surrender crowns Christ Lord. Faith appropriates Christ as Life. Stephen was "full of faith and of the Holy Ghost."

Did you ever see a perfect rainbow? Usually one end is perfect and the other seems to go off into nothing. Looking out over the ocean I once saw distinctly both ends of a rainbow coming up out of the water, as it were, and forming an unbroken arch. Through this beautiful symbol, the Holy Spirit interpreted to me the relationship faith has to grace in salvation as revealed in Ephesians 2:8: *"By grace are ye saved through faith."*

The arch of salvation is all grace from the Godward side and all faith from the manward. God's grace is always perfect. But how imperfect is man's faith! God has provided in Christ all that is needed for a life of habitual spirituality. But to make such salvation experimental, faith must appropriate the provision. Grace provides; faith possesses. Faith makes experimental what grace made potential to every believer.

God tells us that without faith it is impossible to please Him. Some of Christ's severest rebukes were to unbelief in His disciples. To have His presence, His words, His works fail to inspire faith grieved the Lord Jesus exceedingly.

115

You remember when He was in the ship and the storm arose and they cried out in fear. What a word of rebuke He spoke! Even though the tempest raged and the waves dashed high and He were asleep—yet He was there. Why should they fear? Fear and faith are incompatible.

> And he saith unto them, *Why are ye fearful, O ye of little faith?* Then he arose, and rebuked the winds and the sea; and there was a great calm (Matt. 8:26).

At another time Peter was walking on the water at the Lord's command. The wind became boisterous and Peter began to sink. But why should he doubt? Had not the Lord of the sea said, "Come," and did not the power of His protection accompany the command? Doubt and faith are irreconcilable. If we have doubt we haven't faith; if we have faith we haven't doubt.

> And immediately Jesus stretched forth his hand, and caught him, and said unto him, *O thou of little faith, wherefore didst thou doubt?* (Matt. 14:31).

The disciples had crossed the lake after witnessing Christ feed the multitudes with a few loaves and fishes. They were greatly concerned because they had forgotten to take bread. Why should that cause worry? Had they not just seen Him feed more than four thousand people with seven loaves and a few fishes with seven baskets full left over? Would He not be equal to furnishing an evening meal for twelve people if need be? Worry and faith cannot dwell together.

> Which when Jesus perceived, he said unto them, *O ye of little faith, why reason ye among yourselves, because ye have brought no bread?* Do ye not understand, neither remember the five loaves of the five thousand, and how many baskets ye took up? Neither the seven loaves of the four thousand, and how many baskets ye took up? (Matt. 16:8-9).

Oh! how we crowd Him out of our lives by that triumvirate of evil—fear, doubt and worry! Failing health, financial losses, overwhelming burdens, tempests of affliction and adversity come upon us, and we become insensible to His presence, doubt His Word and forget His works.

Some of Christ's sweetest words of commendation were called forth by faith, and strange to say they were spoken to those who knew Him the least. The centurion, whose servant lay sick, appealed to Christ to heal him. Christ promised to go to him. But the centurion answered, "Lord, *speak the word only* and my servant shall be healed." Oh! the joy such faith brought to Jesus' heart and the sweet commendation to His lip, "I have not found so great faith, no, not in Israel."

There is no record in God's Word and no instance in human experience where grace and love have failed to respond to faith and trust. God would be untrue to His nature, which is love, if He failed once to respond to real faith. To some of you such faith may seem impossible. But faith is the simplest thing in the world. Faith is just looking unto Jesus Christ and taking Him at His Word. Why isn't it easy then to have faith? It is because we look at the difficulties instead of Christ, and the more we look at them the bigger they become. They shut Christ out of our vision. Faith in itself has no power whatsoever to save or to keep us, but it links us to Christ who has the power. Let us now consider three ways in which faith operates.

Walking along a wooded path in the mountains of Switzerland I saw an interesting tree. On a steep slope was a tall pine tree with a huge boulder lodged right underneath it, lifting the main trunk several feet from the ground. The tree was fairly sitting on top of the rock, yet it shot staight upward fifty feet. How could such a position be maintained? The secret was not hidden from our view. The roots of the tree had spread themselves over that rock and had gone down, deep, deep into the earth around, so that even the boulder lodged at its very heart could not overturn or overwhelm it.

What a lesson it spoke! Afflictions, adversities, sufferings, sorrows, temptations, trials, doubts, disappointments roll in upon us. How can we go on in peace, patience and victory with such things in our life? Are they not enough to overwhelm us? No, not if faith spreads itself out over them and sends its roots down into the rich soil of God's great, eternal facts.

What are some of these facts? I can mention only a few tonight, but I hope you will

search God's Word and find many more of
them for yourself.

God is love.

> He that loveth not knoweth not God; for
> *God is love* (I John 4:8).

This is one of the greatest of God's eternal
facts, for us to root our faith in. It may seem
as though God had forgotten or that His
hand of chastening were too heavy upon
you. It may seem as though He had closed
His eyes or deafened His ear. It may even
seem as though He were altogether indiffer-
ent to the burden you carry and the heartache you endure. But, friends, it isn't so, for
God is love and the love of God shines as
the brightness of the sun, whether you are
warmed and refreshed by its rays or not.

A Chinese woman came to ask me why she
couldn't win her mother, an ardent Budd-
hist, for whom she had prayed for years and
whose heart had constantly grown harder.
As I studied her face I saw lines which in-
dicated hardness and rebellion in her own
heart. With a little gentle probing there
came a torrent of both tears and words. "God

is unfair; He doesn't treat me right; other mothers can have their children but I have lost my five boys one by one; the last, my baby, died just last month. God is unfair." For a few moments we cried together and then we talked together of the love of God. That love had given the five boys; surely it was love that had taken them back home to Himself. Slowly the roots of that little woman's faith spread themselves over that boulder of sorrow and went down, down, down into this eternal fact "God is love." Then peace and joy came into her heart. "What has happened to you?" her mother asked, the next time they met. "I never saw your face like this before." Then the daughter told her of the rebellion toward God but that now it was gone. From that day the mother was willing to hear the gospel, and in a few weeks had accepted Christ as her Saviour.

God's Grace is Sufficient

> And he said unto me, *My grace is sufficient for thee:* for my strength is made perfect in weakness. Most gladly therefore will I rather glory in my infirmities, that the power of Christ may rest upon me (II Cor. 12:9).

God never promised that the Christian would not have temptations and trials, but He did promise that with every temptation there would be a way of escape, and that with every trial there would be strength to endure. When our weakness is most pressing, His strength is most perfect.

Christ is Able to Save to the Uttermost

Perhaps some of you said last night, "I cannot live a yielded life in Hong Kong." You thought of your non-Christian home, of your social circle with its gaiety and worldliness, of your business life with its temptations to dishonesty and graft, and you said, 'I can't live a yielded life in such surroundings." Yes, you can if you let the roots of faith reach into the soil of this eternal fact, "Christ is able to save to the uttermost." He has both the power to cleanse from sin and to keep from sinning.

Think of the boulders that rolled in upon the life of the apostle Paul: stripes, stonings, shipwreck, perils, ad persecutions of all kinds. But his faith spread itself over all these testings and trials and rooted itself in the eternal facts of God's love, grace and power, thus enabling him to grow up to magnificent spiritual stature. What the glorified Christ did for Paul He stands ready to do for you and me.

FAITH RECKONS ON GOD'S FAITHFULNESS

Our faith may falter but His faithfulness never. Peter failed Christ, but Christ's faithfulness to Peter remained unshaken. The heavenly Father cannot forget His promises nor can He deny Himself by failing to keep them.

> *If we are faithless, he abideth faithful;* for he cannot deny himself (II Tim. 2:13, R.V.).

We may be ready to give up in defeat to the enemy, to lay down our task in sheer discouragement, or even to take our hand from the plough and turn back altogether. But Christ is not dismayed or discouraged. He will not give up in despair. He acknowledges no victory on the devil's part. He has assumed responsibility for us and He abideth faithful.

> *Faithful is he that calleth you, who also will do it* (I Thess. 5:24).

In Switzerland I watched two girls cross a glacier. The path was not marked out; there were great gaping holes in the ice; they were not properly shod with spiked shoes. Yet they tripped along unafraid and in safety, because they were roped to one who knew how to avoid the dangers and surmount the difficulties of that icy path, and they reckoned on the faithfulness of their guide.

Our pilgrim journey is beset with dangers and difficulties, but we need have no fear, for we, too, are roped to a Guide, who is especially appointed by our Father to lead us safely the entire way.

FAITH RECEIVES GOD'S FULLNESS

Are you God's child? Then, by virtue of your sonship, you may be filled with the Spirit. Why, then, do you not possess your birthright? There are three ways an honest man may gain possession of a thing—by purchase, by barter, or as a gift.

Can one buy fullness of the Holy Spirit? Simon the sorcerer was severely rebuked for attempting it. Is there anything we can exchange with God for it? The rich young ruler might have exchanged half of his possessions for the life more abundant, but he went away sorrowful. Have you, perchance, tried to strike a bargain with God, offering Him some odd moments of time, some remnants of strength, some segment of talent, in exchange for the fullness of the Holy Spirit? One way remains by which you may possess the Holy Spirit's fullness, which is to receive it as a gift.

> And hereby we know that he abideth in us, *by the Spirit which he hath given us* (I John 3:24).

What does one usually do with a gift? He receives it and thanks the giver. This is precisely what God wants you to do with this wondrous gift of the Holy Spirit's fullness.

Let me illustrate by an incident which brought this truth to my own heart with fresh meaning. Two Chinese friends, Mr. and Mrs. Wang, came to call upon me one day. Mr. Wang was only a young Christian but he loved the Lord devotedly. What a love for the Word of God also! It was his meat and drink. Seeing this, I was reminded of a Scofield Bible someone had sent me to give to a Chinese friend. I presented it to Mr. Wang, saying, "I see you love the Bible.

Here is a Scofield Bible which I should like to give you." At the mention of a Scofield Bible his face grew radiant and his eyes filled with tears. "Oh," said he, "the other day I saw a Scofield Bible and how I have wanted to possess one ever since! I began to pray for one. I went to a store to buy one but I couldn't afford it."

Mr. Wang decided he could not buy a Bible, and no one had offered to exchange one for anything which he had. Just one way of possession was open to him—to receive it as a gift. And now it was being offered to him. What did he do?

Did he say, "I want the Bible more than anything but *I haven't prayed long enough for it*—just wait until I pray a few months more for it." Or, "*I am really not worthy* to receive that Bible. I must wait until I have made myself a better Christian and am worthy to possess it." Or, "*This Bible is coming too easily*. I think I should do something myself to get it." Or, "You say that Bible is for me, but *I do not feel* that it is, so I think I should wait until I feel that I possess it."

If Mr. Wang had made any one of those foolish remarks I should have been forced to one of two conclusions; either he was not honest and really did not want a Scofield Bible, or else he thought I was not honest in truly offering that one to him.

But what did Mr. Wang do? I wish you could have seen the quickness with which he TOOK that Bible and immediately kneeled down and THANKED God for it. As he rose he began to talk of how he would USE the gift in winning men to Christ.

Have you wanted the fullness of the Holy Spirit? God offers Him in His fullness to you as a gift. What have you done with the offer? Are you still praying for this fullness? Or are you refusing the gift until you think yourself worthy of it? Or are you foolishly attempting through self-effort to make yourself full of the Spirit? Or are you waiting for some ecstatic feeling as proof of the infilling of the Spirit of God?

My friend, if you are telling God that you long to be filled with the Holy Spirit and yet doing these foolish things, either you are not honest and really do not want to be filled or else you do not believe that God is honest when He offers you the gift of the Spirit's fullness.

Are you honest? Do you truly want to be

filled with the Holy Spirit? Then acknowledge the presence of the Holy Spirit within you, and claim His fullness as your birthright. Take the gift, thank the giver, and use the gift immediately in winning souls to Christ.

By an act of faith you may receive the Spirit's fullness. By a constant succession of acts of faith, the Spirit's fullness becomes habitual.

Moody Press, a ministry of the Moody Bible Institute, is designed for education, evangelization and edification. If we may assist you in knowing more about Christ and the Christian life, please write us without obligation to: Moody Press, c/o MLM, Chicago, Illinois 60610.